The Scrum Master Toolkit

The Scrum Master Toolkit

Be the Scrum Master

Every Team Deserves

Al Kraus

Copyright © 2020 Al Kraus
All rights reserved.
ISBN: 9798550113134

To Karen and Julie.
Without your support, none of this would have been possible.

Special thanks to all those who provided valuable feedback
and helped make this body of work possible:
Michael Brashier
Kelly Thompson
Sherry Hall
Kelly Woodfield
Lauren Gibson
Robin Morgan
Rob Evans
Lindsey Jarvis

Contents

Preface i
   Value Proposition: Scrum Master Toolkit ii
Introduction v
Facilitate Group Discussions 1
   Use Mind-mapping for Ideation 2
      Introduce the Activity 4
      Hold the Space Open 5
      Organize, Group and Refine Ideas 6
   Help any group make a decision 6
      Roman Vote 7
      Fist of Five 8
      Majority Voting 9
      Dot Voting 10
      Consensus Voting 11
   Focus the conversation by grouping topics 12
      Six Boxes Activity 12
Facilitate Planning Meetings 15
   Facilitate Standup 17

Three Questions 19
Walk the Board 21
Facilitate Backlog Refinement 22
    Preparation 24
    Team Conversation 25
    Story Sizing 25
    Decomposition 28
    Horizontal Slicing 30
    Vertical Slicing 30
    Follow up 32
Facilitate Sprint Planning 33
    Clean Up Last Sprint 33
    Team Capacity 35
    Building the Sprint Backlog 36
    Tasking the Work 38
    Committing to the Forecast 40
    Trouble Shooting 40
Facilitate Inspection Meetings 43
    Facilitate Sprint Review 44
        Prepare the Presentation 44
        Facilitate conversations 47
        Take notes 47
    Facilitate Sprint Retrospective 48
        Gather observations 48
        Choose a retrospective game and approach 51
        Prepare the room for the event 53

- Run the meeting 54
- Closing the meeting 57
- Follow up 58

Research Retrospective Games 59
- Facilitate SaMoLo 60
- Facilitate Learning Matrix 62
- Facilitate Sailboat 63

Distinguish Between Popular Frameworks 65
- Explain Scrum framework 66
  - Scrum Values 68
  - Scrum Defined 70
  - Contrast with Traditional Approach 70
- Explain Kanban principles 71
- Explain the importance of the Sprint 75

Maintain Processes for Team 77
- Describe Scrum roles 78
  - Scrum Master 79
  - Product Owner 83
  - Team Member 87
- Describe Scrum Artifacts 89
  - Product Backlog 89
  - Sprint Backlog 91
  - Sprint Burndown 92
  - Release Burn Up 93

Coach Your Teams to Improvement 95
- Identify how the Agile mindset drives improvement 96

- Visualize the Work...96
- Inspect and Adapt..97
- Limit Work in Progress..97
- Work in Small Batches..98
- The Importance of Trust...98
- Servant-Leadership..101
- Remove Impediments...102
- Map traditional roles to the Scrum roles...106

Grow a Team Culture...113
- Choose your coaching stance..114
  - Training..114
  - Mentoring...115
  - Facilitation...116
  - Coaching..117
  - Choosing a Stance...117
- Facilitate the team...118
- Communicate our policies..125
  - Working Agreements..125
  - Definition of Ready...127
  - Definition of Done..128

Encourage Team Growth...129
- Identify challenges of self-organizing teams...130
- Describe importance of technical best practices..................................132
- Serve the Product Owner..136

Coach Stakeholders and Leaders..140
- List stakeholder behaviors that support teams....................................141

- List stakeholder behaviors that do not support teams 143
- List benefits lost if Scrum is implemented incorrectly 145

Mentor Others 147
- Mentor Other Scrum Masters 148
- Mentor Non-Agilist 150
- Engage in the Community 151

Embrace Continual Learning 153
- Engage in self-study 154
- Plan for future Certification 155
- Research the career journeys through Scrum Master 157
  - Path of Technical Excellence 157
  - Path of Leadership 157
  - Path of Coaching 158

About the Author 159

References 161

Photography Credits 163

End Notes 165

Preface

*"Many ideas grow better when transplanted into another mind
than the one where they sprang up."*
~ *Oliver Wendell Holmes*

Do your meetings drag on with little to no productive outcomes? Do team members recoil when they are asked to attend a Scrum event? Is the team just not "getting it"? Does the team keep trying to revert to their old way of working? How often do you have to really work to drag improvement ideas out of them? Do you aspire to obtain the "white whale" of a hyper-productive team? It's time to take matters into your own hands and gain the knowledge and insight you need to achieve your goals.

Through this material, it is my goal to share information about how you can become the Scrum Master you wish you had, and that every team wants but they just don't know it yet. In the Scrum Master Toolkit, we will work together on how best to bring a group of people together to be a team, make your meetings efficient and productive, coach your teams to be self-reliant, and to push them to be far better than you, or they, ever thought possible.

A great Scrum Master is always learning. Not just about Agile, but all of the different disciplines that go into it. The role of the Scrum Master is one of the most commonly misunderstood roles within the current corporate world. Scrum Masters are routinely held responsible for the value delivered by their team(s), while staying out of the team's solution space. A good Scrum Master leads their team through the influence of being a servant-leader. A great Scrum Master inspires a team to want to be their best selves and to always be better tomorrow than they are today.

*"My dear, here we must run as fast as we can, just
to stay in place. And if you wish to go anywhere
you must run twice as fast as that."*
~ Lewis Carroll "Alice in Wonderland"

Successful Scrum Masters rely on skills and techniques from professional facilitation, coaching, mentoring, presentation, training, and team building, just to name a few areas. This toolkit is a major step on your journey, a way of ensuring you have the skills, knowledge and tools to propel you to success.

Value Proposition: Scrum Master Toolkit

Much of the better practices shared among what is a relatively organic, global Agile community of practice is experiential, dependent upon the depth and breadth of your instructor, coach or mentor. The value I personally offer includes my experience serving many different Agile teams over the course of fourteen years. I have been honored and blessed to directly learn from giants in the industry, such as Jeff Sutherland, Lyssa Adkins and Daniel Mezick. I have shared my training approach with numerous Scrum Masters, helping them discover new and exciting ways to iterate their own mastery.

We are about to embark on a journey to learn how to effectively facilitate meetings, coach your team to empowerment, increase productivity, and become the Scrum Master that every team deserves. Based on your experience, you can probably relate to the following common questions:

- How do I bring this group together to be a team?
- How can I help the team adapt to a Scrum approach?
- How can I coach the team to hold itself accountable?
- How do I make the meetings fun and effective?
- What are the next steps for me, both personally and professionally, as a Scrum Master?

We will cover these concerns and more, starting with how to keep meetings on track and productive. After, you will learn how to gain influence within your team to enable you to coach them towards improvements. When you do, your teams will experience the following things:

- Teams that hold themselves accountable and feel empowered.
- Team members are driving ideas for improvement.
- Team members are happier and look forward to coming into work
- Engagement in meetings, creating innovative solutions to issues.
- Meetings become a source of energy for the team instead of a drain.
- The team will be more productive than they thought they could be.

A common misunderstanding about the role of a Scrum Master is that their purpose is very basic, focused solely on keeping the lights on for a team. However, there is so much more to this critical role. For instance, Jeff Sutherland states in his book, *Scrum: The Art of Doing Twice the Work in Half the Time,* that "Scrum done correctly can lead a team to expect 400-1800% productivity gain." The Scrum Master role is critical to making this happen. We will explore what to look for and provide you with a strong foundation to become, not just a good Scrum Master, but a great Scrum Master.

Introduction

Agile software development has been around since the mid-1990s. Pioneers in this emerging field gathered in 2001 and created the Agile Manifesto to compile the lessons they learned while experimenting with better ways of creating software. These visionaries brought together different ideas on how to increase productivity and efficiency. The ideas became the basis of the Agile philosophy using the Manifesto as its foundation. The Agile Manifesto has four values and twelve principles. The values are included here:

We are uncovering better ways of developing software by doing it and helping others do it. Through this work we have come to value:

Individuals and interactions over processes and tools
Working software over comprehensive documentation
Customer collaboration over contract negotiation
Responding to change over following a plan

That is, while there is value in the items on the right, we value the items on the left more.

From these simple values, many different Agile frameworks and approaches have been developed. Frameworks specify processes and practices used to encourage and support Agile values. A commonality of different Agile approaches is that they enable companies from across the world to deliver valuable, higher-quality software faster than with any method from before the Agile movement.

We in the Agile software-development community have learned our lessons, and it's time for us to become teachers and help others learn from our successes and mistakes. In this book, I strive to introduce the critical role of Scrum Master to help the next generation get a jump start so that they can better change the world that we work and live in.

Beginning with facilitation and moving through the processes and roles. We will talk about the different skills you will use to help coach your teams to success. Finally, we will conclude with suggestions on how you can continue your own learning journey.

I hope you will join me on this grand adventure into the world of the Scrum Master. Come see how the role can be one of the most fulfilling opportunities available to us. And see how, with these lessons, you can help your department, or possibly even your entire company, develop into a learning organization that is continuously improving.

Facilitate Group Discussions

Bring any group to a quick and decisive decision

Y ou are likely wondering why I am starting a book about being a Scrum Master with facilitation and not about Scrum. The reason is simple. If you understand how to facilitate meetings well, even if you do not fully understand all the ins and outs of Scrum and how to implement the framework, you will be able to offer added value to your teams. This is the first and most basic skill that a Scrum Master can use to build rapport and relationships with team members. Rapport is critical to our being successful as we start to coach more of the underlying Agile principles. Do not fear; we will cover Scrum information in depth in Chapters Five and Six.

Meetings can be some of the most productive work that we can do. Reading this, you are likely thinking that I obviously have not been present in the same meetings as you.

Over the years, you'd be surprised at the meetings I've taken part in and how much I can relate to your situation. Likely, the meetings you have previously attended could have used some help from the skills and techniques that you are about to learn. First, we will discuss some skills that can help you facilitate any group discussion.

Groups need to come together for conversations for many reasons, the most common being idea generation and decision-making. Facilitating these types meetings, will create a foundation we can build on. In addition, you will learn how to keep any conversation on track so that the group does not spend valuable time repeating information or talking at cross purposes.

Being seen as the person to help a group efficiently run conversations is one of the first of many steps that will foster groups requesting help from, not just any Scrum Master, but you by name. This facilitating skill goes a long way in validating the importance of the Scrum Master role as a change agent who drives improvement and helps everyone achieve their goals.

Use Mind-mapping for Ideation

Mind-mapping is a technique used to create and articulate a bunch of ideas, very quickly, from a group of people. As a flow of consciousness exercise, people can allow their imaginations to run wild. Most groups are surprised by the volume, depth and diversity of ideas generated the first time they participate in a mind-mapping session. The term mind-mapping is sometimes interchanged with brainstorming; however, there is a difference between mind-mapping and brainstorming. Both are flow of consciousness exercises; however, mind-mapping is generally a little more structured than a brainstorming exercise. Whenever you are currently using brainstorming; you can easily substitute with mind-mapping.

> ## Mind-Map
>
> A mind map is a graphical way to represent ideas and concepts. It is a visual thinking tool that helps structure information, helping you to better analyze, comprehend, synthesize, recall, and generate new ideas. Just as in every great idea, its power lies in its simplicity.[i]

Scrum Masters can apply mind-mapping as a powerful tool to assist the team. It can be used to quickly populate an initial backlog for a new team, the team is starting a new project, or if the team needs to breakdown a larger feature request. Mind-mapping can be deployed to quickly break larger ideas down into smaller, easier to handle, pieces that can then be talked through in more detail by the group, and at a later time.

So, what do I mean when I say "flow of consciousness"? The most common example of this is word association. One person says a word and another responds with the first thought that comes to mind. Often times when we attempt to generate ideas, we filter our own ideas before we write them down or speak them aloud. Lots of extremely good ideas are thrown away this way. Some of the best discoveries often come when someone starts off with something like "I know this is crazy but, …". That idea itself might not be a home run, but it may trigger something for someone else who adds a completely new thought into the process. It is extremely important that when you facilitate these sessions, that you help people feel safe so that they are open and willing to openly share any thought, no matter how ridiculous it might initially seem. Once ideation is done, there is sufficient time to review and filter ideas.

> ## Time-box
>
> A time-box is any amount of time set aside for a specific task. When the designated amount of time is up, the task is done no matter where the task is at that time.

> Time-boxes are extremely helpful for discovery activities and to create regular check-ins. Scrum uses time-boxes in most of the activities throughout the framework. They can also be used to set time aside for a conversation, keeping it focused and productive.
>
> It is important that, as a facilitator, you pay attention to ending the time-box on time. Without this discipline the group will not improve their ability to focus conversations and the value of the time-box is lessened.

Most mind-mapping sessions are time-boxed. Time-boxing is important because the ideas are usually generated so quickly a group can generally run out of ideas in a matter of minutes. Don't worry, there will be plenty of output for the group to process afterward.

A common time-box for the idea generating part of the activity is ten minutes. Of course, you may end brainstorming earlier if the flow of ideas runs out. Generally, going longer than ten minutes will not generate more or better ideas, as people tend to start over thinking. With introduction of the activity and idea grouping, you should be able to generate a good deal of information in approximately thirty minutes.

Introduce the Activity

Many teams are not familiar with the mind-mapping process when you start working with them. The setup for a mind-mapping session is critical to gaining the most innovation from the group. This can be accomplished in different ways. Regardless how you choose to proceed, there are three components necessary in order to successfully prepare the group.

- First, establish the foundation for the process and describe the expected outcome. Explain the topic or theme to be discussed is placed in the center of the board to provide space on all sides for idea generation. Describe the purpose of the initial ten minutes, which is intended to generate as many ideas as possible about the main topic.
- Second, it is important to understand that all ideas, no matter how unusual or unconventional, are welcome. You never know what idea or thought can

be triggered by random, free-thinking conversation. Now is not the time to respond or react to ideas. A bad idea does not exist within this portion of the activity. This is the power of a shared flow of consciousness.
- Third, we discourage self-filtering of ideas and thoughts. Encourage the contribution of any and all thoughts to the group. The more we can contribute to the group knowledge and ideation, the better the results will be. Remember, we will filter later.

Hold the Space Open

Once you have instructed the group about how the activity works, you are ready for the fun part. As stated, place the topic in the middle of the board using a sticky note, dry erase whiteboard or shared virtual board. There are also specific tools for this type of activity. When working with a team, especially if they are all in person, a big dry erase board is perfect, others prefer to use sticky notes so they can more easily group items later.

Once you have the topic in the center of the space, draw a circle around it. Then ask the group the question they should be addressing in relation to this topic. This question will depend on the context and purpose of the meeting.

If you are focused on ideation for a large feature to be completed, you should share the feature with as much detail that already exists, and then ask them to break down the work. This will generate pieces or components of the work that may or may not need to be done; and, this approach will also likely generate questions that need to be answered. Of course, once you set the stage and ask the question that start the conversation, don't forget to start the timer for ten minutes. As quickly as you are able, write all ideas on the board. Drawing as many lines connecting ideas to any other related idea or the topic that you can while keeping up with the flow of ideas. You are only adding lines for ideas that you, or the group, know are connected. If possible, attempt to group related ideas as you record them, which will assist in later conversations.

Done well, mind-mapping is very powerful. Facilitating this activity appears very easy, yet it is deceptive in its simplicity. I worked in a past life with a Product Owner who had watched me facilitate several mind-mapping sessions. He believed that he understood how to facilitate mind-mapping himself. When he first started the mind-map, he stumbled several times, learning on the spot the degree of difficulty, especially when it comes to not interfering with the flow of consciousness generated by the group. His shortcoming, at the time, was attempting to dig too deep on each idea that was generated – a lesson learned.

Organize, Group and Refine Ideas

When the ten-minute time-box has ended, or the flow of ideas dwindles, point out to the group exactly how many items they generated in such a short amount of time. Give them a couple of minutes to look over the thoughts and ideas they created together. At this point, you could drive organizing ideas or you could empower the team to self-organize around the board and draw their own lines to connection and group ideas. Items are grouped that are related to each other in order to better organize them for the team to use. If the group decides that any idea might need to be discarded, they can do so once they have talked about it together and agreed.

Once the group has finished organizing ideas, a list can be generated and prioritized. There are several ways that prioritization can happen. If the ideas generated were to start a backlog, the Product Owner may choose to prioritize the list themselves. Other times the group might be asked to make a decision and they can utilize a decision-making approach, which we will discuss later, to complete this initial prioritization together.

Help any group make a decision

There is nothing more discouraging than leaving a meeting thinking that everyone is in agreement, only to later find out that the group was not. I once found myself in a position where we had several people in a meeting to discuss the results of an experiment to embed people with a particular skill (subject matter experts, or SMEs) into all of our Scrum teams. The issue was that there were only two specialists to be embedded into fourteen teams. So, we conducted an experiment for three sprints to see if the two SMEs could be embedded into one team each, while serving as a point-of-contact for the remaining twelve teams.

At the follow up meeting, we reported that there was no perceived benefit of embedding the two specialists over just having them assigned as a point-of-contact. We left the meeting thinking the experiment was over and the SMEs would simply work with teams based on need, requests, etc. However, their manager left the meeting thinking the experiment had been a success and pushed to embed the SMEs on the remaining teams. As you can imagine we were very concerned. It is practically impossible for two people to be embedded and accountable for the Sprint commitments of fourteen teams. This example serves as a reminder of why it is so important to ensure everyone is in agreement and has an equal level of understanding when decisions are made.

Not only is it important for everyone to understand what the decision was, but that once the decision is made, everyone agrees and supports the decision. If people who disagree with the decision decide to ignore or countermand it, then there really was no point for the group to work toward a common understanding. When a group is making a decision, everyone has a voice. Every participant's contribution and point-of-view should be included in shared knowledge information gathering so that the best decision possible can be made. Once reached, all should abide by this collective decision.

One of the strengths of a facilitator as part of the conversation is their ability to quickly guide a group to a clear, concise decision resulting in takeaways, such as action items. Not all decisions are mission critical, and therefore, they do not require the same amount of group buy-in.

Now we will explore five different effective decision-making techniques, including how to use them and, more importantly, when they are a good choice for the decision at hand. Whenever you call for a vote using any method, it is always helpful to restate the proposal being voted upon as clearly as possible. If in doubt, clarify the purpose and shared understanding before calling the vote.

Roman Vote

The Roman Vote is one of the quickest ways to help a group make a decision. It is used in order to make a fast decision while not interrupting the flow of a conversation.

Once you have stated the topic and clarified any remaining questions, count to three. At the end of the count, each person will use one hand to display one of three signs.

- Thumbs Up – indicates agreement with the proposal.
- Thumbs Down – indicates rejection of the proposal.
- Flat Hand or Sideways Thumb – indicates neutrality, or no strong opinion, on the proposal and the person will go along with what the rest of the group decides.

Roman Votes are useful for 1) deciding to continue a time-boxed conversation, 2) asking if a group is ready for a break, or 3) any decision where it is not critical that everyone completely agrees.

Fist of Five

Like the Roman Vote, the Fist of Five is another quick way of gaining feedback and decisions from a team, extracting more information from participants as it is not a straight "yes" or "no" input.

Once you are ready to call the vote by clearly stating the proposal to be voted on, you count to three. Each person then holds up the number of fingers on one hand of how strongly they agree with the proposal.

- Five fingers indicate enthusiastic approval.
- A closed fist, no fingers, indicates strong disagreement.
- Generally, if everyone uses three fingers or more the proposal is considered agreed upon.
- If anyone two fingers or less, then there needs to be more conversations on the reason that they are not interested in the proposal. You can ask them what it would take for them to vote with a "three" or greater. This typically leads to a brief discussion and refinements in the proposal. Then, you can call for the vote to be taken again.

I have used Fist of Five to check-in with the group, asking them how they feel about a topic, their happiness level or choosing where to go for lunch. I have also used this technique when tasking a group of people to define standards, such as coding standards or working agreements. In fact, in Chapter Eight, I mention how I use a Fist of Five when creating working agreements to ensure team buy-in.

> ### Working with quiet teams
>
> Both Roman Vote and Fist of Five are great when working with quiet teams or teams that have not yet become comfortable with speaking out. Everyone becomes engaged in a way that feels safe, and helps increase psychological safety for the team. We will discuss more about this in Chapter Eight.

Majority Voting

Majority Voting is the method most people know from political voting. There are three different Majority Voting standards: Simple Majority, Lesser Majority, and Greater Majority.

- Simple Majority is simply the option with the most votes.
- Lesser Majority requires greater than fifty percent of the vote in order for the proposal to pass. Note that when the vote is between two options, a Simple Majority vote is effectively is the same as a Lesser Majority vote. The only difference comes into play when there are more voting options.
- Greater Majority is typically seventy five percent of the votes are for the proposal, which can be seen in action if you watch votes within the United States Congress.

Voting can be conducted as closed or open voting structures. An open approach can be done quickly by a simple show of hands. A closed structure allows people to vote without fear that their vote will be held against them. This is typically the approach when elections are held to decide between candidates.

How you facilitate voting will, of course, depend on whether you are conducting closed or open voting. If a closed vote, a typical approach would be to have everyone write their vote on a small sticky note. Collect all the votes without looking at them, and mix them up. Pull one sticky note at a time and read the vote. Then record the tally of each voting option.

Open voting is easier in that all you have to do is verbalize each option and ask people to raise their hand if that is the option they chose. You simply count the number of hands to tally votes.

After all the votes are tallied, if a majority has been reached, you have your decision. If the majority has not been reached, then the group might need more conversation and then additional votes until a majority is reached.

As you can guess, it may be possible to end up in a seemingly endless loop. So, each time you start the vote on the same topic or decision, you should consider removing the option that received the least votes. Votes are then redistributed across the remaining options, thus increasing the chance of a majority being reached.

Similar to the Fist of Five vote, you could ask the group what it would take for them to agree to the option with the most votes. This can also increase the speed of reaching a majority. If you believe that a stalemate, or tie, is possible, it is best to gain agreement from the group ahead of time on how to proceed if a majority is not reached.

Majority Voting can be a more time-consuming process, but when the decision is critical it may be necessary. Other voting techniques are better options unless you really need a majority of the people to agree a decision. Reiterating for emphasis, once a decision is reached, everyone needs to abide by it, otherwise the decision is weakened and therefore, less valuable.

Dot Voting

Dot Voting is a very quick way of getting a lot of information from a group, especially helpful when there are a lot of options from which to choose. Another good application for this voting technique is to define initial prioritization from several items.

The setup for Dot Voting is fairly straight forward. Once you know how many items there are to be voted upon, divide that number by four and round up, to determine the number of votes each person will have. For example, if there are ten ideas, then divide ten by four and arrive at two and a half, which rounds up to three. This means everyone will get three votes. Explain to participants that they can assign some or all of their votes on any given option, but they can only use so many votes in total (three in the case of the above example). I would be amiss if I did not mention that there are some facilitators that divide by three instead of four. This is mostly preference, so use what makes sense to you. Votes can be given in a variety of ways. I have used checkmarks, tally marks, and even poker chips if in person. Whichever method you chose, make sure people know how to assign their votes.

After everyone has voted, you will tally the votes for each option. If you are using this technique to make a decision, such as determining a team name, then the name with the most votes wins. If there is a tie, eliminate all ideas except for the options that are tied for the top, and repeat. Likely everyone will only get one vote on the second round. If the team is voting to create a prioritized list, then the items can be organized by the order of the number of votes for each. If two items have the same number of votes place them next to each other, as the final prioritization should be done with more conversation from the group.

I have experienced Dot Voting as working well for prioritization, for example when a team is starting a new project and they need to quickly populate their backlog in order to start working. This approach also worked for helping a team decide on a name, where to go for lunch, or countless other decisions involving several options.

Consensus Voting

The toughest of the voting styles to help reach a decision is Consensus Voting because everyone needs to agree with the decision for it to be accepted. When used with a small group of people, this can be achieved, and actually should be a goal whenever conducting a majority voting type of approach. As desirable as consensus is, with large groups of people this is very difficult to achieve. The Majority Voting described earlier will likely be a better fit.

Consensus Voting is conducted just like Majority Voting and can be done both closed and open. However, if all the votes are not designated toward one single option, the group needs to continue their discussion until they think they can attempt a successful voting outcome.

There is often a great deal of compromise done during Consensus Voting conversations in order to make each of the options more appealing. This is much easier to do when there are fewer selections, such as only two voting options. Depending on the topic, the conversation can become intense, so as facilitator you will need to keep the focus on the main topic. Even though you are unlikely to use this technique as a Scrum Master, it is important to know about it is an option.

Focus the conversation by grouping topics

I worked with a team on a mind-map of possible improvements. Within ten minutes, they developed more than thirty ideas. These items were all over the place, from Donut Fridays, to creating an automated pipeline, to releasing work faster and easier. I led them through an activity of grouping their ideas into buckets and then asking them to decide which bucket they should work on first. This helped the team determine the next actionable item much more quickly than reviewing the entire list all at one time.

In this chapter, we have discussed multiple decision-making techniques to help groups move toward action more quickly. One way to be more efficient while incorporating more ideas is to group like items together. Then voting can center on which grouping is the most important, and from there the team can examine just the items in that group if further detail is needed.

Grouping like ideas is important for more than just voting or brainstorming activities. Often when you are gathering information from multiple people, you will have some inputs that are simply different ways of saying the same thing. Other times, grouping is an efficient way to eliminate a group of items from a current discussion. These items can be discussed at a later time, as applicable.

Six Boxes Activity

One grouping technique is an exercise called Six Boxes. When you have no idea how many ideas will be generated during a discussion, but you do know that you need to arrive at a limited number of main objectives to choose from, this is a great technique.

Six Boxes is exactly as it seems…you guarantee that ultimately there will only be six boxes from which to choose from. I have seen this approach used effectively to generate ideas for types of improvements that might appeal to customers. The group ideated on common pain points, which were then grouped using Six Boxes. The result was a means to connect ideas and the output was six areas for customer improvement. These areas were then prioritized, solutions generated, and new items were added to a backlog.

The Six Boxes Activity is a great approach when working with a group on silent or quiet ideation on a specific topic. If the group is small enough this can be done as an individual exercise, or you can breakout into small groups. Here I describe a particular way of leading this activity, but once you understand the basics, feel free to change it to best suit your needs.

- Write down the theme of the ideation.
- Under the theme, draw out six boxes, a two by three table.
    - Draw the six boxes large enough to accommodate multiple sticky notes.
    - Do not label the boxes: we do not know at this time what information will be included.
- Give the group(s) a time-box to generate three ideas each. On average, ten minutes is good. If the team generates more ideas, then ask each person to choose their top three for the next stage of the activity.
- Once the time-box has ended, ask a volunteer to read their three ideas. As they read each idea ask them to choose a box to place the sticky note. Most likely the first person will put one stickie into three different boxes, which is perfectly fine.
- As each person reads their ideas and adds them to boxes, you will quickly run out of boxes.
- At this point, facilitate a conversation to see how the existing stickies could be moved around to be grouped with similar ideas so that there is an open box for the new, additional idea. Grouping can be at any time if the participants think ideas should be moved around.
- Once a box has four or five sticky notes in it, you can pause the reading of new ideas, and ask the group to define and name the box. Once named, this box is

set and should not change again. Continue to add ideas and naming boxes until all the ideas are placed on the board and all boxes have been named.

- The restriction of the number of boxes will force a conversation within the group, helping them to think of different ways to find similarities between ideas, and forming groups of ideas at a higher level.
- Once all the boxes have named, you can lead the group through a relevant activity, such as prioritizing a list of epics for a backlog.

Facilitate Planning Meetings

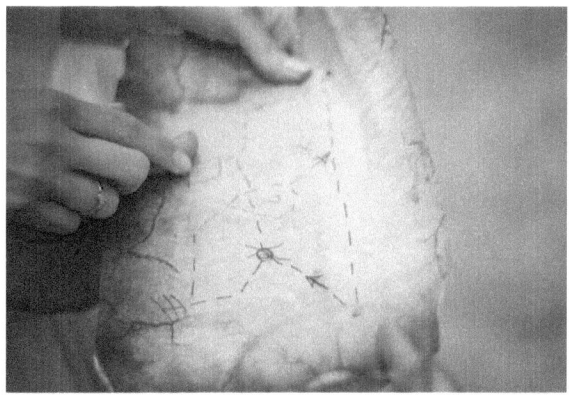

Effectively facilitate planning meetings to maximize team productivity

Facilitating group discussions and decision making are key tools to keep sharp in your tool belt. No matter how good you are with them, you can always be a little better. Applying these tools in the Scrum meetings is the bread and butter of the Scrum Master role. At one point or another, every team will get to the point of seeing the meetings as something that takes them away from doing the work. This is especially common when there are meetings from before the transformation, in addition to the Scrum meetings, that are still continuing and taking up the team's time. Done correctly, the Scrum meetings should be the only meetings team members should need to be in on a regular basis, with an occasional additional meeting here and there. As such it is vital for you, as a Scrum Master, to be able to run these meetings as efficiently as possible and get your team back to work.

In order to accomplish this, it is important to make the team understand a couple of fundamental concepts. First, meetings are not a distraction from work, they are work. If a team leaves a meeting without feeling like they accomplished something, then you need to investigate why and attempt to fix it. It could be that meeting preparations were not done ahead of time, or that conversations dragged on when they could have been aligned quicker. Your goal should always be to have people leave the meetings with more energy than when they came into it. This is extremely hard to do, especially in every meeting, but it is a great goal for you to strive for. The second is making sure that the team understands the "why" of the meeting. This seems straightforward, but as time goes by, people forget and you will need to remind them of the purpose of the event again in order to keep it efficient.

One of the best ways to ensure your meetings are hitting the mark is to ask your team for feedback. You can do this informally as the opportunity presents itself, or formally either in the retrospectives or by sending a survey. Remember the more information you take in, the better you can customize for the team. An extremely important point to remember, especially if you are working with multiple teams, is that it is not about you, it is always about them. Don't force a team to do something because it is easier on you to have all your teams work in the same way. Let your teams work in the way that is best for them.

Scrum is a game

When Scrum is implemented correctly it has all the characteristic of a good game.[ii] These characteristics include:

- Participation is optional
- The rules are clearly stated
- The goal of the game is understood by all
- There is a way of measuring progress throughout the game

> Approaching Scrum in this fashion makes it more enjoyable for you and your teams. It is easier to become more accepting of mistakes as learning opportunities. In fact, the subtitle of the Scrum Guide written by Ken Schwaber and Jeff Sutherland is *The Definitive Guide to Scrum: The Rules of the Game.*

To support the execution of this, we will walk through each of the Scrum events and talk about the "why", as well as give steps on how you can facilitate each meeting. These steps are not intended to be the only way that these meetings can be run. Instead they are intended as an example of how they can be run. We will also talk about the key components of each that you should ensure are present no matter how you customize the facilitation for your teams. Keep in mind these basics: get them in, get the work done, and then cut them loose. In this chapter we will concentrate on the planning meetings. We will cover the inspection meetings in the next chapter.

Facilitate Standup

The daily standup is likely the most misunderstood and abused meeting of all the Scrum events. It is a fifteen-minute meeting. It is kept at this time limit to ensure the conversations are concise and do not wander. We have all been in a standup meeting that, when it was over, everyone left the room feeling drained and still unconnected. This is normally because the meeting has lost its purpose and needs to be reset. I have also seen that when the team is able to use this as a daily planning, they leave the room feeling energized and ready to get the work done.

Why we do things is often more important than what we do. If we have the wrong 'why' in mind, we are more likely to make decisions that will take us away from our intended target. Anytime you find your meetings are losing their way, take the time to re-ground the team in what they should be attempting to accomplish. Ask the team if they feel they are achieving that goal; and if not, ask them how they think they can accomplish the goal better going forward. This re-grounding of the team will typically inject more energy into the meetings as people are reminded of why they have that meeting and that they have the authority and responsibility to own their own effectiveness of them.

The biggest issue we see with the daily standup is the tendency to revert to a status meeting. This can be especially easy if the manager of the team members is in the room during the standup. Almost all Scrum events are open, so anyone can observe, but it will be your responsibility as the facilitator to make sure that guests remain observers and that there are not too many of them, as it can distract the team from accomplishing the goal of the meeting. If observers become too much of a distraction, you may have to ask them to leave. The main difference between the standup and a status meeting is the focus on what was done and the level of detail required. In a traditional status meeting, you are giving an update of everything you did the previous day. This often makes people feel they need to justify how busy they were and list all the things they worked on. During a standup, the team talks about what was done, but only so much as how it helps plan for the day ahead. The key here is to focus on planning for the day ahead more than all the details from the previous day.

You may be asking, if the standup is not a status meeting, what is it then? It is in fact a daily planning meeting where the team is deciding how they can get the most work done before the next standup. Instead of status, there should be coordination. Team members should feel comfortable asking and giving assistance to each other. This includes stepping out of their primary skillset if it moves the work forward. Everything within Scrum is focused on getting more value delivered. This daily coordination is no exception.

> **Agile Coaching Principle:**
> Focus on the idle work not the idle workers
>
> Find ways to keep the work moving forward, with team members doing anything they can to best accommodate this forward movement. Sometimes the most productive thing is to pause, take a breath, and work on improvements to how the work is done over bringing in and starting additional work.

The Scrum events are setup to allow the team to focus most of their time on delivery of the work, with less distraction from outside noise. We will discuss this in more detail when we talk about coaching the team. The important piece of it for now is a concept of just-in-time planning. You will find as we progress through the events, each one has a different level of detail that is applied, and that we only apply the level of detail necessary for the stage the work is in.

> **Just-in-Time Planning**
>
> We need enough planning right now to allow us to continue to work at a steady pace. Any additional planning would run the risk of needing to be thrown out if priorities change in the future.

The daily standup is the most detailed planning the team does. It is completed at the task level of the work, allowing the team to organize themselves in the most efficient way of completing as many tasks and stories within the time-box they have before the next standup.

Three Questions

The three-question format is by far the most common. It is the format described for this meeting within the Scrum Guide created by Ken Schwaber and Jeff Sutherland. It is also the easiest way to get people new to Agile to understand while they are learning this new way of working. As with most things, there is more than one way to run this type of meeting. You can take these descriptions I give you and modify to your taste to help the team. Whichever format you chose, it is always helpful to display the team's sprint board to help encourage and focus the conversation.

Once everyone is in the room, physical or virtual, the meeting can start. Hopefully, like all meetings this will be on time, though sometimes people arrive late. You will need to get the team's agreement on how important punctuality is. This will be discussed more in Chapter Eight about team policies. Select, or let the team select, someone to start off.

Then each person in turn will talk with progression going clockwise around the group. On each person's turn, they will answer three questions:

- ➢ What did I do yesterday?
- ➢ What will I do today?
- ➢ What has blocked me from getting work done?

It is important as facilitator that you keep people on track, remember you only have fifteen minutes for the entire daily planning and likely many people that need to talk. If someone starts to get into the weeds, ask them if we can put the rest of that conversation into the parking lot so we can keep the meeting on track.

> **Parking Lots**
>
> When most meetings end, there is normally conversations that continues. This could be in the hallway as people walk away from the meeting or in the parking lot as people are heading home. I have often found myself still talking to someone an hour or so after an event was officially over because of good conversation.
>
> In Scrum we often use this concept to keep meetings on track. Make sure that you write down all topics put into the parking lot as the meeting progresses. Once the main portion of the meeting is over. Inform the group that the meeting is officially over and you are going into the parking lot. This allows members that do not feel they need to be involved in the more detailed conversations to leave, while the interested parties can have a more in-depth conversation.
>
> To allow for this, it is sometimes a good idea to schedule the stand up for half an hour. Finish the standup in the first fifteen minutes and have the time scheduled for fifteen minutes of parking lot if needed. It is important that the team understands that it does not make the standup half an hour.

Once all the team members have had their turn, ask the Product Owner if they have any updates for the team that might affect their plan for the day. After the Product Owner, it is your turn. Clarify any impediments that you heard the team bring up in this meeting and give updates on any previous impediments you looked into so that they know you are working on them. I recommend you end with asking the team if there is anything you can do to assist them to be more productive as a closing question. Take notes on their reply and end the meeting. Oh, don't forget the parking lot if you have anything in there.

Walk the Board

In some ways the Walk the Board format is similar to Three Questions. However, the focus is different. In walk the board, you display the sprint board to the team, and progress story by story in the order of importance from top to bottom. For each story ask the following questions:

- ➢ What did we do as a team to complete this story yesterday?
- ➢ What can we do as a team to move this story to completion?
- ➢ What is preventing this story from being finished?

This format is my preferred one for teams that have been together for some time. It focusses the conversation on what we do as a team instead of what we do as individuals. This is a subtle, but important distinction. It also groups all conversation about a particular story together instead of scattered throughout the turns of team members during the three-questions format. The fifteen minutes time-box still applies. If you do not get to all the stories by the end of the time, it is okay as the team discussed the most important stories for the sprint which is what they should be focused on.

I prefer the focus on working as a team that this format gives. It is important to understand that it can be more difficult to facilitate. This is because it is easier for the team to hide work that is not aligned to the sprint just by not talking about it. As the team discusses each story, you will need to try to notice if anyone is not talking. Once all the stories have been discussed, if you have marked that someone still has not spoken up it could mean that they were working on something not in the sprint. Do not be afraid to ask them. A simple, "Hey, Joe I might have missed what you were doing today, can you repeat what story you are going to be working on?" Another good idea is to also ask the team if anyone is working on anything not on the board. Remind them that the sprint work is the priority and needs to come first. As a final question, you can also ask if everyone has something planned to work on for the day. These questions encourage the team to pay attention to who is helping on the sprint backlog, who is being distracted, and who is not pitching in. Remember, it is your responsibility to help the team hold itself accountable, not just to act as an enforcer.

Facilitate Backlog Refinement

Once you can get a team to hyper-productivity, you will never forget what that feels like. I had been working with a team for some time called Abby Normals when I first experienced this. They were building a prototype to combine two massive gaming platforms together and only had a couple of months to prove it out. They all knew the deadline and were bought into it. The Product Owner and I sat with the team to ensure we were always readily available. They reached a point that they would routinely refine fifteen or more stories in a fifty-minute refinement session. Even with this, they would run out of ready stories on the backlog for each sprint. They would plan their sprint with the velocity of the previous sprint each time. And each time they finished that work, brought in more work and finished that, increasing their velocity more. Their productivity shot through the roof because they were always in alignment and the work to be done was clearly understood by everyone.

Backlog Refinement, previously referred to as grooming, is a best practice to allow teams to be more efficient in their sprint planning. It allows teams a chance to see the work that will be in their near future and to discuss with the Product Owner in order to make sure the work is truly ready to be started when they start their next sprint. We will discuss more about what it means for a story to be ready in Chapter Eight.

"planning is everything, the plan is nothing."
         ~ Dwight Eisenhower

Refinement is a great example of this quote. It is about the conversation, not about a definitive plan. Plans change, but the conversation is still valuable.

> ## Placeholders for Conversation
>
> Stories are placeholders for conversations; they are not intended to be mini-contracts. They should contain enough information so that everyone can reflect on the conversation, with important points from the conversation referenced and no more. When in doubt, the team should talk about it, not go by the black and white of the story.

The refinement meeting is also where the Product Owner gets a chance to really shine. Most of the time, the Product Owner will be the one driving this meeting. They will share their screen, and add notes to the stories as the meeting progress. This allows for active listening on behalf of the Product Owner while the team can see the changes that are added to the story and voice any modifications that are needed. If you drive this meeting, the team is seeing how well you understand the conversation, while the Product Owner might have a different take that is not discovered until the team does the work. This is not to say that it cannot work with the Scrum Master driving, you will just need to be cognizant of this and ensure that everyone is in alignment. It is important to note no matter who is driving this meeting, you still own facilitating it to ensure the meeting is efficient and valuable to the team.

Preparation

Refinement is a meeting that starts before the team walks into the room. The best refinements follow a common pattern. First, the Product Owner needs to be prepared. They must have the stories to be discussed ready for the teams with as much information as they can. Second, the team needs to be prepared. The Product Owner should send the stories to the team ahead of time, and the team should look them over and start preparing any questions they may have on them. It is important to do this before the meeting starts. Different people read and process at different speeds. If this is done during the meeting, the meeting will drag for those on the team that read and process quickly as they wait for the members that take a little more time. Those that are slow often attempt to be quicker because they feel bad for holding the meeting up; unfortunately, when they do, they often miss things. By doing the appropriate preparation ahead of time, people can feel comfortable taking the time they need to read and process without delaying anyone else. Third, the Product Owner should verify that the backlog is in the correct priority order so that as the team refine the stories, the most valuable are done first.

Like any Scrum event in order to help the team get the most out of this meeting you may have to remind them of the purpose of the meeting and help them keep the conversations on point. If the team needs to ideate ideas, do that in a story jam meeting where you can mind-map their ideas. Use refinement only for that purpose. Daniel Mezick in his book, *The Culture Game*, applies a theory of treating all meetings as games in order to increase engagement. To do this, as stated earlier, we must make sure the rules of the game are clearly understood by everyone. It might sound like over kill to cancel a refinement meeting to schedule a story jam in its place. But the action sends a signal to the team members to change their expectations and preparations for the meeting, which will make the meetings go better.

> **Story Jam**
>
> A story jam is a meeting specifically arranged to have a team do ideation in order to generate as many story ideas as they can. They typically use the mind-mapping activity previously described in Chapter One.

Team Conversation

Once the preparation is done, it is time for the meeting. Like all meetings, if you can get whoever will be driving the meeting to be there a little early so that the technical concerns are out of the way, it helps streamline the meeting and gets to the good stuff faster. Start the conversation on the highest priority story that has not yet been sized. You might have to go back to one that has been sized if information has changed on it, in which case remove the size and treat it like a new story. Once the story is up, and if everyone came prepared, the team should be able to jump quickly into the conversation.

As the facilitator for the meeting, your main role is keeping the conversation going and focused on where it needs to be. This is a difficult balance between letting the team discuss enough detail to appropriately size the work while not getting caught up in the weeds of details that they will not need until they pull the story into a sprint and start working on it. If you happen to come from the domain that the team works in, distinguishing between these two sides becomes a little easier. What becomes harder for you is staying out of the solution space. It is acceptable to ask questions, but the team owns the solution. If you are not from the knowledge domain of the team it is of course much easier to stay out of their solution space, however, you will need to learn to pay close attention to the flow of the conversation in order to tell if the team needs you to interject to keep them on track and focused.

This monitoring of the conversation is made easier if the Product Owner is driving the meeting. Once it appears that the team has asked their questions, it is time for them to attempt to size the story. This can be initiated by the Product Owner or the Scrum Master.

Story Sizing

The best practice for sizing a story is to use Planning Poker. This is an activity where everyone decides on a size, relative to other items in the backlog, using the Fibonacci or modified Fibonacci scale. Once everyone has a number, all numbers are revealed simultaneously. This decreases the chance of a single voice dominating or influencing others in the sizing of the story.

Fibonacci numbers

The Fibonacci number set is a set of numbers based on observations from nature. Each number in the sequence is the sum of the previous two numbers.

Fibonacci: 1, 2, 3, 5, 8, 13, 21, 35
Modified Fibonacci: 1, 2, 3, 5, 8, 20, 40, 100

Using this number set accounts for the understanding that the bigger the story being sized, the vaguer it is and the less we need pin point accuracy on the size. This keeps the team focused on the work and not going back or forth on is this an eleven or a twelve. If it is bigger than an eight, make it a thirteen and move on.

Relative Sizing

You might be asking why we don't just estimate in days or hours. The truth of the matter is that humans are notoriously bad at estimating how long something will take to do. The more complicated and complex the work, the less likely a time estimate will be useable for planning and predictability. We are however, extremely good at doing relative sizing. This is bigger than that. This is about the same size. Using this technique improves the predictability of the team and therefore will inspire more trust in the roadmaps they agree they will be able to deliver on. It is important to remember that the size placed on the story is an abstract combination of the effort, complexity, and risk of a story.

For anyone who is not yet convinced on the benefit of relative sizing over time sizing, ask yourself this question:

> - If a cross-functional team puts a size estimate on a story, whose time should they estimate?
>   - The person that the story falls within their specialty?
>   - The newest member of the team that is still getting up to speed?
>   - The average person?
>   - How do you calculate what the average person would be able to do?
>
> The truth is that time estimation feels more natural and familiar, and it is. However, it is not normally the right tool for estimating at the story level. We will revisit this when we talk about tasking stories in Sprint Planning.

> **Agile Coaching Principle:**
> **Group thinking over specialist**
>
> A team will get better estimations once they start sizing as a team instead of just letting the specialist size the work. This increases the usefulness of the conversations as each person has a different perspective. It is also important that during refinement we may not be certain who on the team will do the work. It might be the specialist, but it might not be.

Often the team will come up with a range of numbers. It will be your role to help them come to agreement on a number as quickly as possible. There are several different approaches you can use for this. Typically, a team will have a standing agreement that if the sizing is split between two consecutive numbers, e.g. three and five, that they automatically take the larger number. This agreement can speed up sizing a great deal for these smaller differences. Other times, the gap is larger. One approach I use most often is to ask whoever had the smaller number why they chose that number. Once they have explained their reasoning, I then ask the person with the highest value why they chose their number. During both explanations, it might be uncovered that there are more unanswered questions that might need more conversation. If that happens, let the conversation continue until they are ready to vote again. If the second vote still ends in a range, you can start the conversation by asking the people on the extremes what it would take to meet in the middle. This might include adding acceptance criteria, decomposition, or even some additional research that can be done before the next refinement session. Another approach that should be agreed upon by the team ahead of time is that if the second vote still has a range, that the group takes the average number. Many people believe, based on their understanding of statistics, that taking the average for the estimate is not significantly different than getting the entire group to agree and it is much quicker. Sometimes, it is more expedient to not size a story at this time and to allow the team to do some quick investigation before returning to size the story in the next refinement to resolve the bigger unknowns.

Decomposition

When teams first start sprinting, they normally have a good deal of difficulty fully grasping refinement. At first, they don't see the need to break the work down. Then they do, but don't understand how to break it down. After that, they become overly dependent on using Spikes as the only way of doing decomposition. A spike story is one that is meant to quickly discover some information to assist in further story refinement. Typically, this would be when the team determines two or more different technical approaches that might work. You might have a spike story to make a quick proof of concept of each approach to establish which path the team should go down. They are meant to be short, deep dives for knowledge. The knowledge, not the proof of concept, is the value from the spike. The proof of concept should be thrown out. Because the team knows the proof of concept will be disposed of, they are more likely to do the bare minimum to get the information. This reduces the amount of work overall that is going to get thrown out while still allowing the team to make an informed decision. Once the team learns of spikes, they tend to default to using these types of stories whenever there is a question about how to implement a new story. Spikes are powerful tools but should be used only when the other methods are exhausted. An important point for now is the two different approaches to decomposition.

Break down work with SPIDR

When a story is sized too big for the team to be able to complete within a sprint, then it should be broken down. There are many different ways to decompose a story. However, this is a very difficult task and teams generally need a good deal of help in the beginning to figure out how to do this well. One technique from Mike Cohn is SPIDR.

S – Spike (First only because it makes a cool acronym)
P – Path
I - Interface
D – Data
R – Role/Responsivity

Spike – A quick deep dive for knowledge. Should be used when there are multiple approaches to developing the solution and the team needs to pick a path before, they can proceed.

Path – Decomposing a story by paths is to break down a story based on the path the user will take through the system. For example, a path might be if the user does everything as designed while another path might be if the user cancels out half way through.

Interface – Breaking the story down by interface is by the way different components of the system communicate with each other. There is an example below about decomposition based on the credit card backend that the system needs to use.

Data – This is breaking the story down based on some form of data used by the system. A simple example of this would be different interface languages that the user might use. If the end solution is being designed to use eight languages, first completing the functionality with one language so you can get feedback on how it works before you translate it into the other seven languages.

> **Role/Responsibility** – This is breaking a story down by the type of user in the system. For example, the way a customer uses the system is different than how an admin would use the system.

Horizontal Slicing

Horizontal slicing is breaking a story down by the stages that make it up. For example, if we needed to accept a credit card payment on a website, we could break the story down like this:

- ➢ Create the payment webpage
- ➢ Create the database to hold the transactions
- ➢ Create connections to merchant services
- ➢ Create controller logic to connect all pieces and process transaction

As you can see, horizontal slicing is a natural approach to breaking a problem down. This is also similar to a waterfall approach that many people are familiar with. The issue with this approach is that if it takes the team a sprint to do each bullet point listed above then even if the stakeholders in the review love the look of the page it still cannot be delivered to production until all parts are done at the end of the fourth sprint, assuming no delays. That is, it delivers no value to the customer during the first three sprints. Not to mention that the third story is the bulk of the work as every type of card that needs to be accepted has its own merchant services backend requiring a slightly different connection.

Vertical Slicing

Vertical slicing is a way of breaking a story down into small functional pieces. In the example above, we could use the Interface option from SPIDR to break down the story like this:

- ➢ Accept MasterCard payments
- ➢ Accept Visa payments
- ➢ Accept Discover
- ➢ Accept Amex

With the first story, the team would need to build the webpage and the database but then only have to worry about one connection to a merchant service. At the end of the first sprint, if the business wishes, they could roll the code to production and begin accepting MasterCard payments. Sure, you can only accept MasterCard, but you can accept MasterCard users six weeks earlier than with a horizontal approach. Visa would be earlier by four weeks. Since these two types of cards are the majority of the credit cards on the market, you are getting return on the investment of production earlier and in a much more Agile way.

While working with one team just starting out, I described the difference between horizontal and vertical slicing. They listened intently then went back to using horizontal slicing. During the next sprint, the topic came up again. And again, after listening to my explanation, they again went back to using horizontal slicing. Sometime later in yet another refinement, in the same situation, I again explained the difference between the approaches. This time after listening to me, they paused and thought about it. You could almost hear the gears clicking and then a sudden light bulb turning on. The response this time was "of course we should break it down that way, why would we ever do it any other way." True story.

Agile Coaching Principle
Vertical Instead of Horizontal Slicing of Work

Whenever possible, break down stories in such a way that you can deliver a small piece of functionality that works from front to back and delivers value to the customer and will allow you to get feedback on what was produced so that you can increase the value during the next sprint.

> Although horizontal decomposition, "layering", is more intuitive, it prevents getting actionable feedback on how the system works for the customer until all the pieces are complete. Therefore, each small part delivered does not deliver real value to the customer until everything is done, which might make it harder to pivot if the approach was off to begin with.

> **Curse of Knowledge**
>
> The curse of knowledge is that once you learn something it becomes extremely difficult to remember what it was like to think any other way. This is critical for Scrum Masters to understand, because we suffer from it. The more we come to understand Agile and how it can help teams, the harder it becomes to remember a time when it did not make sense and waterfall was a better solution.

Follow up

Once the time for the refinement is up, end the meeting. It is an important tool to start to build trust with the team to always end meetings on time. They come to depend on it. After the meeting, you might want to follow up with the Product Owner to ensure they got everything they needed and that they have a record of the questions the team needs them to answer for the next refinement. You can also follow up with anyone on the team that took an action item to do a quick investigation to help the refinement of a story to ensure that have it on their list. This investigation should only be to be able to size the story and should not take a large amount of time.

Facilitate Sprint Planning

There are a couple of tricks to running a successful planning meeting. I gained the honor of learning these by having the meeting go wrong more often then I care to admit. From attempting to plan without a backlog or replacing the backlog right before the meeting, to running out of time without tasking all stories, I have seen it all. There are lots of moving pieces and any one can go askew. In this aspect, it is sort of like meditation. When things don't go as planned don't beat yourself up, just re-focus and continue. Good advice for all facilitation but more so for Sprint Planning in particular.

Some of the things I described can be done ahead of time if the team keeps things up to date. I will describe the facilitation in case it all has to be done during the meeting just to make sure that it all happens. The main purpose of planning is for the team to decide how much of the top of the backlog they feel they can commit to attempting to deliver and to create an initial plan on how to attack the work. If you do not use this specific approach but still reach the same goal, awesome. If not, then you have a roadmap to start from.

Clean Up Last Sprint

Often times when the team gets into planning, the first thing we need to make sure is that the previous sprint board is cleaned up. If you are fortunate enough to walk into planning and the previous sprint is all cleaned out and you don't need this step, make sure to celebrate this with the team. This is definitely something we want to encourage more of.

If not, there are a couple of likely things that need attention. The easiest are tasks and stories that are completed and accepted but not updated on the board. All you have to do with these is close them. You can also include a gentle reminder that if this was done ahead of time, you would not need to use valuable meeting time. Other times some of the stories are not quite done. Before you just move them into the next sprint there is some work to be done. First, ask the Product Owner if these stories are still top priority or should they be put back on the backlog. If the answer is the backlog, go ahead and move them there. If you will be carrying over to the next sprint we need to sort through an issue.

To help illustrate this, let us assume the story to be carried over was an eight-point story and the team has a capacity of twenty points for a sprint. If we are carrying over the story, we need to ask the team how much work is left. The way I normally phrase this is, "if the remaining work on this story was a full story, how many points would it be?" I have had teams come back with every possible answer from half a point to twenty points. Why is this number important? It is the number you should use for planning purposes. Do not change the value on the story as that was the initial estimate. We need to know how much of the team's twenty-point capacity for next sprint will be consumed by this carry over work. Again, for our example let us assume there are three points left. Write this down on a side note somewhere so we can use it later.

Online Tools

Most online tools have an extremely helpful feature where it will sum the total point currently in the sprint. This takes most of the math out of planning as the total is increased as you add stories to the sprint. If this is the case, you can short cut the math of carry over stories by calculating the amount of work already completed and just subtracting this amount from the tool generated total.

Example:

Let's say the team currently has thirty points displayed as included in the sprint, with a carryover story which was originally eight points with an estimated three points remaining. This means the amount of work completed on the story was five points. By subtracting five, the amount of work completed, from the thirty, shown in the tool as the total point in the sprint, you can see that the team has twenty-five points of work planned in the sprint.

Why do we not just use the original eight points for planning? It will be more apparent if I exaggerate our scenario a little more. Let us use a team that has three stories to carry over with original estimates of three, five, and eight. If their capacity is still twenty then their next sprint will be these three stories and another three to five points of work. If the three carry over stories are barely started, this works out fine. However, if these three stories are almost done, but they just could not cross the finish line by the end of the sprint, e.g. they each have one point of work left. Then what you have is a sprint that appears full at first glance but is really just six to eight points of work. The three carry over and the three to five additional points pulled in. This is less than half what the team can handle and they will likely need to bring in more work during the sprint. By using the number based on the work remaining, we get a better idea of how much work the team can pull in without under or over planning the sprint. Once planning is done, we can throw these numbers out, as they are for planning only. The stories still keep their original estimates.

Why don't we just change the size of the story before bringing it into the next sprint? Great question, glad you asked. Since we use the average velocity of three to eight sprints to determine how much the team feels they can bring in, changing the story points on the story effectively discounts all the work that was done the previous sprint. This will skew their velocity metrics and make it harder for them to predict how much to plan for.

Team Capacity

Once the previous sprint board is cleaned up have the team discuss any time off, or other constraints, that will take away from their ability to apply effort towards the sprint. It is important for the team to keep this in mind as they plan out the sprint. You don't want to encourage the team to take in their full velocity of work into the sprint if half the team is on vacation for most of the time. This does not need to be tightly accounted for, but having each person discuss their time off will keep it fresh in everyone's mind.

After the team has discussed their availability, show them their velocity chart. We will discuss velocity charts more in Chapter Six. The important part for now is that the average velocity for the past three sprints is a good indicator of what the team is likely to be able to do this sprint. Now that the team has their past performance, in the form of average velocity, and their capacity for the current sprint, ask them for a target range of points they would like to plan for in this sprint. I prefer a range than a single number as it makes the conversation a little easier as you ask them for which stories to pull in. Occasionally, the team will be a little stubborn and persist on giving a single number. When they do, convert it to a range by doing plus/minus two. Confirm with the team that this is an acceptable target range for the sprint.

Building the Sprint Backlog

Now that we have a target range, we can start adding stories. Ask the Product Owner for the sprint goal. As the team goes down the backlog of available work, they should keep this goal in mind and pull in only stories that align with the goal.

> ### Sprint Goal
>
> The Product Owner should come to the sprint planning with a sprint goal in mind. This is a focused goal to deliver value to the customer. The team will use this as a filter to determine which stories to bring in to best reach this goal.
>
> Occasionally a Product Owner will come with a goal with a good deal of conjunctions. You can coach them to be more focused by helping them put the goal into the User Story format.
>
> As a <customer>, I want <goal> so that I can <benefit>
>
> This should focus the conversation on a goal for the customer. When the goal is made up of several goals, it will encourage the team to shard their efforts and it will take longer to get everything done.

Before we bring in additional work, add the total of any points from carryover stories and compare to the target range the team provided. This allows time to finish that work. Then open the team backlog. This should already be in priority order; however, I still prefer to confirm with the Product Owner that it is in the order they want before starting. Once confirmed, proceed down the backlog asking the team if they are comfortable bringing in the top story. If for any reason the top story cannot be brought in, for example, because there has a dependency that needs to be resolved or it does not align to the sprint goal, continue with the next story. As each story is brought in, add the points for that story to the sum of the points already in the sprint. Keep the team updated on the total number of points of work in the sprint as you go.

If the teams bring stories into the sprint that do not align to the sprint goal, then there is an increasing risk that the goal will not be met by the end of the sprint and the customer will not see the value promised. A great deal of the culture that is created by Agile exists because of the increasing amount of trust created by predictability and improvements. The sprint goal is the best way for the team to communicate to the business what value they are planning to deliver for the customer. If this goal is not met because of non-related work brought into the sprint, the team starts to erode some of the trust they have built up. This is why it is critical to encourage the team to try to stay focused on the goal. Once met, the team can negotiate for whatever they want to bring into the sprint with the Product Owner.

Sprint Forecast and Release Dates

Often times the team will be put under pressure to over-commit to the sprint because of the pending deadline of a release. Encourage them to not over-commit. It helps no one in the long run. The team should be aware of the deadline and should be professional about trying to hit it. Coach them to only pull in what they feel they can deliver without heroic effort. During the sprint, if they complete work early they can pull in additional work as needed. This is a more realistic approach to pushing towards a date than unrealistic sprint commitments that the team cannot deliver on. Missing the sprint commitments will erode the predictability of the team which also reduces the trust that the team can deliver what they say they can.

There are definitely times when heroic effort is required. These should be the exception and not the rule. If the team has to step up, then after the release there should be a retrospective to determine why the extra effort was needed with a goal of preventing this from happening in the future. Remember, the goal is to set a pace that the team can function at forever. Extra hours, nights and weekends are not a sustainable pace and will eventually burn the team out. It is also a case of diminishing returns as the longer someone works in a given day, the more tired they get. The more tired they get the longer

> it takes to get work done and the more mistakes get made. The team is at its most productive if they can get enough rest each night to come to work refreshed and ready in the morning.

Once the total points in the sprint reach the target range, confirm with the team that they are good or if they would like to see if they can complete more. Once the team feels they have enough work pulled into the sprint, it is time to task the stories that have been added to the sprint.

Tasking the Work

For each story in the sprint, ask the team what needs to be done to complete the effort. As they call out tasks, add them to the story. Some Scrum Masters prefer to estimate the tasks as they add them. I prefer to add all the tasks at once and then add the estimates after. The reason is to not interrupt the flow of consciousness of the team as they figure out all the work that needs to be done for the story. Whether you estimate as you go, or once you have all the tasks, make sure that all tasks have an estimate. Unlike stories, tasks are normally estimated in hours. This is because the work to be completed by the task is smaller and clearer than a story, as such the team's ability to estimate will be more accurate for planning.

> ### Team Communication
>
> Some teams will resist putting estimates on tasks or sometime even doing tasks at all. This is common on teams that still view the work in silos. Make sure the team understands the benefits of tasking so that others on the team can more easily help to complete the work.
>
> Estimations have a couple of different benefits for the team. One is that it allows for a more detail sprint burndown, discussed more in Chapter Five. It also allows for a double check on the story point

> size of the story. If the hour estimated for the tasks is drastically different than stories with a similar size, you should confirm with the team that they still believe in the estimate. Finally, the estimated backlog of tasks can be used as a sanity check on the amount of work pulled into the sprint. If the total estimated hours for all tasks is greater than the hours available in the sprint, there is a risk that the work will not be completed by the end. The team can use this additional knowledge to see if they need to adjust their plan for the sprint.

After all the tasks have been added and estimated, the team might decide that the initial estimation of the story was incorrect. By having the conversation to create the tasks, the team now has additional information on how the work will be done. If they wish to resize the story, this is their last chance to do so as once they start the work the estimate should not be changed. If they discover the size was wrong while they are working it, they can discuss in the next retrospective what they missed and plan to avoid the issue in the future.

> ## Assigning Tasks
>
> Different teams will work in different ways. My preferred method would be to leave all tasks unassigned until someone pulls them into progress. However, it is not about me but about them. As such, some teams prefer to assign tasks during sprint planning. This is still okay as long as it is the team assigning the work and not the Product Owner or a manager. If the team does pre-assign the work during planning, make sure they are looking to see if this needs to be rebalanced throughout the sprint as they work on the backlog.

> **Agile Coaching Principle**
> Plans are useless, planning is everything
>
> The most important part of the planning event is the planning itself. The conversations the team has, how they breakdown the work, and create an initial plan are invaluable. This plan might and will likely change as they progress through the sprint, which is why we have the daily standup events to help with this re-planning based on more up to date information.

Committing to the Forecast

The final stage of the planning is comparing the rough estimate of the time the team has for the sprint and the total estimated hours. This is a simple sanity check to ensure that the amount of story points the team pulled in is doable. If the team chose to change the story point sizes of any stories or after the hour comparison, they might wish to pull in additional work, or push a story back to the backlog. If they pull in more, follow the steps above to get it ready. Items pushed back to the backlog can simply be moved there. Make sure the team still has the stories they need to meet the sprint goal in the sprint.

Once the team appears to be good with the sprint backlog, the final step is commitment. Ask the team, including all team members and the Product Owner, if they are good with this forecast. Call for a quick Roman Vote. If everyone is okay then planning is done. Since the team has been having conversations throughout, this should be a formality. Every once in a while, there will be need for further conversation. Have them talk it out and call another vote. It is important that the full team agrees to this forecast as they will all need to work towards it. The last thing to do should be to activate the sprint in the tool and let the team get started on the work.

Trouble Shooting

This event, more than the others, has a lot of moving parts. Because of this, I think it is important to discuss some common ways things could become derailed. A couple of these include running out of time in the planning timebox and teams that resist pushing themselves to ensure they complete every sprint. I will talk about some ideas that you can do in both of these situations.

When the time you have set aside for planning runs out and you have not finished all of the planning activities, you have to address the issue from a couple of different angles. The first angle is what to do right now. There are two main options, though I am sure you will come up with more. The first is to inform the team, get the commitment on the sprint, and have the team complete the planning on their own. This might include adding tasks and estimates on their own. The second option is to schedule another planning meeting for later in the day. Either way you should be able to get out of the situation for the day, but now you need to think about how you got into it. You will need to determine why you ran out of time. If the reason is that you had not scheduled enough time, then you should adjust your scheduled meeting to be longer. Remember that the Scrum guide recommends eight hours of planning for a four-week sprint with proportionally less for shorter sprints. If you are trying to complete planning in one hour for a two-week sprint, then likely you are not giving the team the time they need to properly complete sprint planning. If the amount of time is good, but the team did not stay focused or allowed themselves to go down too many rabbit holes, then you may have to bring this up during the next retrospective to get the team's buy-in to trying to stay on task so that they can complete the plan in the time they have.

Remember that the goal of any team should be to find ways to deliver more value faster. Most of the time this is about finding ways to eliminate waste in their processes but sometimes it is convincing them that they can do more than they think they can. If the team has not failed a sprint, described below, within the past four to five sprints, then there is a good chance that they are not pushing themselves enough to discover just how much they can accomplish within the timebox of the sprint. It is easy for a team to get into a rhythm and decide to plan the same amount of points each sprint. If you notice this, then a gentle push to attempt to get them to stretch a little might surprise them that they can do more. Remind them that failing a sprint is a learning opportunity, not a sign of failure.

Failing a Sprint

A simple metric can be used to understand how well the team can predict what they can deliver over the course of the sprint. If the team does not complete at least eighty percent of the work they committed to, then the sprint can be considered failed. When this happens, the team can discuss why it happened and see if they can discover ways that would have allowed them to complete the work on time. This is a great way of learning by identifying areas that hold the team back.

Some people resist using the term "failing" as it normally has a very negative connotation. However, I believe that we need to embrace our mistakes and learn from them because we will always learn more from our mistakes and failures than we will from our successes. By using the term in such a learning way, we should make progress in removing the stigmatism on the term.

Facilitate Inspection Meetings

Effectively facilitate inspection meetings to maximize continuous improvement

In the previous chapter we covered the three planning meetings in the Scrum framework: Stand Up, Backlog Refinement, and Sprint Planning. We will now talk about the inspection meetings. These are the opportunities for the team to inspect how things are going, and to innovate new ideas of how to make improvements. There are no unimportant meetings. I do have to admit that my favorite meeting is the retrospective that we will cover in this chapter. An important part for both of these meetings is that you should strive to come out of both of them with ideas for improvement and action items whenever possible.

Al Kraus

Facilitate Sprint Review

There are countless ways of facilitating the Sprint Review. The ones I enjoyed the most were setup like a Science Fair. We would have all teams presenting at the same time. Each team would prepare a five-minute demonstration of what they built that sprint. The stakeholders would circulate amongst the teams and ask questions for greater detail as desired. Doing things this way helped everyone in the building see the great work that the teams were doing. Remember for non-IT people, a lot of what IT people do is "magic". This has the effect of helping to boost team morale as well as allow time and space for getting additional feedback.

The more standard approach to a sprint review is a single team review with the team presenting the work they completed during the sprint. Even for this approach there are several variations, help the team chose the best one for them or feel free to tweak this approach to best suit their needs. Of all the Scrum events that a Scrum Master facilitates, the sprint review is typically the lightest lift. That said, make sure the team understands that the review is critical to demo the solution they are building and to get feedback to improve it for the customers.

Prepare the Presentation

To begin with you need to make sure the team understands that the sprint is a time-box to get work done and then to get feedback. Even if the work is accepted as is, after the review there are always lessons to be learned to improve both the solution and the process the team used to build it. There are times that teams get caught up on trying to make sure that they look good at all cost. They end up spending large amounts of time making sure the presentation is perfect. However, the review is for feedback, not status or evaluation of the team, and should be more about working solutions than on a pretty PowerPoint presentation. If the team is taking longer than an hour or two to prepare for the sprint review, remind them that they could be using that time to get more value delivered instead of working on a presentation that will not help them get any more information than what they would have in an hour or two.

> ### Agile Coaching Principle
> #### Fast feedback is better than polished junk
>
> Teams can waste a great deal of time polishing up a review to make everything appear to be better than it actually is because they fear what will happen if the work they did is not approved of. However, this time takes away from actually doing more work. If a rough sketch allows for the same amount of feedback on the approach and only takes a fraction of the time, then it is a better approach as the team can then spend more time building the solution. This goes directly to the Agile value of working solutions over comprehensive documentation. Do not gold plate the solution by adding in more than is needed. Work towards a minimum viable product so that you can deliver faster. This includes not just the solution itself, but also the presentations of the solution as you build it.

There are a couple of key elements as well as some optional ones that a sprint review should have. Remember this is one approach, tailor to suit. A Sprint Review should start with the Product Owner announcing the sprint goal for the sprint. This allows for the audience to put context into the work they will be shown. It should then include all the completed work. Work that has not yet been completed should not be shown as it does not meet the definition of done which the team established. The definition of done is simply a list of achievements that every story must meet in order for the team to consider work done. We will talk more about the definition of done in Chapter Eight. The review should end with the Product Owner sharing what they think the sprint goal for the next sprint should be.

> **Agile Coaching Principle**
> Anything less than 100% is not delivered value
>
> Any piece of work that has not completely made it through the team's work flow is not delivered value. We cannot deploy to our customers if the quality of the solution has not been verified. We cannot deliver to our customers if the training materials have not been created. If we cannot deliver to our customers, then value has not yet been created. There is potential for value that is all. The sprint review should concentrate on the value delivered only. It is then a business decision on whether there is enough value built up in the solution to deploy to the customers. The business owns that decision, but the team owns ensuring that everything they say is done can be deployed whenever that decision is made.

Once the team has determined how they will present the necessary items, they could choose to include some additional items. For some of these, they will rely on you to produce the items for them. The team could choose to show some of their metrics, like their velocity chart, release plan burn-up charts, or list the improvements they have made to their process to help speed up their workflow. We will discuss these charts more in Chapter Six.

Once the plan for presenting the information is complete, the team should work out who will talk about which part of the presentation. You may need to help facilitate this conversation to keep it on track. Help them determine how they will transition between presenters.

While the team is working out the presentation details, confirm the invite list for the review. Make sure everyone the team would like feedback from is on the list; these are the stakeholders and customers for the solution they are building. Then you can update the invite with the updated agenda that the team gives you for the presentation and send it out.

Facilitate conversations

Make sure you get to the room ahead of time. It can be useful if conference rooms are at a premium to book the room immediately before the review to ensure that the team has time to setup. Start any necessary technology required for the review. You want to make sure that when the team starts their presentation there are no obvious technology failures like not being able to connect to the video conferencing for the meeting.

Once the meeting is setup and the team kicks it off, you should step back. It is the team's time to shine, let them. Be prepared to help keep conversations on track throughout, but let them lead. This is an important time to build the bond between the Product Owner and the team as they are all presenting the completed work.

Take notes

As the review continues, make sure that you are prepared to help them by taking notes. They are likely concentrating on presenting. This is an easy way to help them concentrate on that. Make note of any important feedback that the team will need to follow up on. Make sure you also note who gave the feedback as this may help the Product Owner prioritize the request, and the team will know who to follow up with if they need more clarity.

Other import things that can come up during the conversations are new ideas or key questions that need to be answered. Both of these will need further investigation and will likely be added to the backlog and prioritized along with any other existing work.

Following up with the team after the presentation and sharing the notes you took for them will help build that relationship between you and the team. The stronger you can build these relationships; the easier it becomes to do deeper coaching as time goes on.

Facilitate Sprint Retrospective

Of all the meetings that we facilitate, the retrospective takes the most preparation to facilitate successfully. In my opinion it is also the most important because this is where we help the team to drive continuous improvement of their process. This is the opportunity for the team to pause and inspect how they are working and generate hypothesis on how they can make improvements to their workflow so they can increase the value they can deliver.

My technique begins right after sprint planning. Throughout the sprint, I note down my observations so that I can remember specific examples. I add the metrics for the sprint to this list of ideas. The day of the retrospective, I choose which retrospective game I will play with the team based on what I feel is the most important observations I think should be discussed. Immediately before the event starts, I do a couple of facilitation techniques to pump up my energy. This is vital, as keeping the energy in the room up, is key to keeping engagement. High levels of engagement allow you to drive the team to action.

In all the previous meetings, I have gone into detail on how you could facilitate the meeting. I will not do so for retrospectives right now. I will cover the key components that should be in all retrospectives, but not a detailed walk through. This is because I feel this topic is so important, I dedicated all of Chapter Four to go into not one, but three different games that you can use to help the teams find improvement ideas.

Gather observations

In order to properly coach a team, you need to be recording your observations throughout the sprint. You don't want to rely on your memory right before the retrospective to recall important parts. This is especially important if your observations are on something that the team, or individuals on the team, might be resistant in acknowledging. These are the times you will need specific examples and metrics to back up the observations. Luckily you will not always need that level of detail before sharing your observations with the team, but there will be times you need it.

We will cover many of the types of things you should be looking out for with the team in Chapter Eight. As a Scrum Master, you need to attempt to always be hyper-observant of your team. Yes, if you miss something it will likely come to your attention later, however the sooner we see it, the faster we can head it off and the less likely it will become a big issue. It can be very rewarding to be seen as the person that can bring the team back together when everything goes wrong. You get to shine in the spot light and everyone knows you brought them back together. However, you will hear me say this over and over; it is not about you, it is about them. It is much better to be able to spot issues before anyone else and solve issues before anyone even notices there was an issue. Acting in this way, the team avoids the loss of productivity they would encounter from having to fix a major internal issue.

> ## Hyper-Observant
>
> The ability to actively observe a group or team in order to identify issues or complications before they become impediments for the team. This could be noticing a clue that there is a personality conflict between team members or that there is a bottleneck in the team's process of getting work done. The sooner you can notice an issue and address it, the less impact that issue will have on the team.

A long time ago, I came up with an analogy that explains this. Think of a team like a Broadway show. The team is the cast. If everything goes right, they get a standing ovation. If everything goes very right, they bring the writer, the Product Owner, out on the stage and they also get a standing ovation. When this happens and the team is in the spotlight, no one notices the stage manager. That's the Scrum Master. The stage manager is who is in the spot light when the props cannot be found, the trap door opened under the lead actor, or one of the backdrops fell at the wrong time. We should not want the spotlight as it means something is not going well. When we do our job well the team shines and that should be our goal.

There are several categories of observations you should be looking for. How is the team doing on accepting the Agile values underlying the processes they are using? How are the team members working together? How are they working with the Product Owner? Are there additional best practices that should be pointed out to them? Most importantly, how are they interacting with each other socially? Are things tense or is everyone getting along? Is there someone that controls all the conversations?

Most people that come to the Scrum Master role are problem solvers by heart. As soon as we make the observations, we jump into problem solving. It is okay to attempt to find the root cause of the observations as well as come up with possible ideas on how to fix them. However, what you do with this thinking depends on the team and where they are in their Agile learning journey. If the team is just starting their journey, then you will likely be able to share your thoughts and improvement ideas. However, as the team continues on their journey, it becomes imperative for you to be able to hold back. Holding back on the solutions, not the observations, always share the observations.

> **Telling the difference between Scrum Masters**
>
> Generally speaking, you can tell how experienced a Scrum Master is by the ratio of how many questions they ask versus how many solutions they share. A Scrum Master, newly minted and freshly ordained, expects that all teams should do things by the book and any deviation from this is something to be worked on and fixed. They share their knowledge to help the teams, but do so in a way that comes across as telling the team what to do.
>
> On the contrary, a more experienced Scrum Master will share observations and then ask the team questions to help the team create their own solutions. Often times, the solutions the team come up with will be better than the ones the Scrum Master did. Regardless, the team is more likely to implement a change they came up with than one they are given.

You will likely have to limit how many observations you share at any given time. My rule of thumb is all of the good and one of the constructive. We need to celebrate as many successes as we can. We don't however need to dwell on all the areas of improvement we need to work on; having one area to focus on at a time is enough.

Once you have your observations, you cannot forget your metrics. We will talk more about the metrics and how to interpret them in Chapter Six. Gather them up, so that you can present them to the team if needed to help share your observations or to answer questions. You want to always look like you are prepared for anything that the team asks you for.

Choose a retrospective game and approach

A retrospective game is a structure and imagery that you can use with the team to help them inspect and adapt on their processes. There are lots of retrospective games out there that you can choose from. In the next chapter I will introduce you to three of them. Sometimes you will have a gut feeling for which to run, other times you will choose based on your observations and what you would like to guide the conversation around.

> ### New Box
>
> One game that I use when the team appears to be in a rut, is a game I made up called *New Box*. It is basically just a mind map session with a twist. You ask the team to describe everything that would be in their perfect work environment. They should assume they have unlimited time, people, money, and other resources to achieve this goal state. I normally throw out some silly ideas like balloons in the team area, pancake Fridays, silly hat Tuesday, etc. in order to really break them out of the mental box they have themselves in. Once the ideation is complete, do a quick round of dot voting to find out which ideas are the most important to improving the work environment for the team. Then ask them what they can do, within what they can control, to take a step towards this state.

Now that you have your game chosen, there are several approaches you can take depending on the team and the locality. Preferably, your team is co-located. When everyone is in the same room it can be easier to facilitate and keep everyone engaged. These approaches can be modified slightly for distributed teams as well. The end goal of all of these approaches is to increase engagement and increase psychological safety so the team can have the conversations they need to make improvements.

> **Psychological Safety**
>
> Psychological safety is what we call it when people feel safe to voice their true opinions and do not fear reprisal for them. It is imperative to build and maintain with your team. Without this, the team cannot have the sometimes-difficult conversations they need to have in order to make real breakthrough improvements. Lack of safety can also cause information and risks to not be talked about which could cause problems to go unaddressed causing drag on what the team can accomplish. During the retrospective, it is imperative that we keep safety in mind for everyone. Part of this is in how you take the notes from the conversations the team has. Since psychological safety is so important for the team to have during the retrospective, it is why we generally do not encourage and sometimes resist having a manager in the room during the meeting. This is not always an option especially with some of the hybrid roles we will discuss later. The important point is that when managers are in the room, people tend to be more careful with what they say and that in itself can limit the team's potential to find growth opportunities.

When you are working with a team that is comfortable speaking out, you can have them all call out ideas while you record them on a stickie. This is a good way to keep the energy up in the rooms as the team is helping you to do so as they engage. Whenever possible, you should stand while facilitating as it helps you maintain your energy level. If you are working with a very shy or timid group, have them write their ideas down on small stickies, collect them, and read them off. With truly experienced teams you can hand off the marker and let someone on the team write the ideas as the team calls them out, or read off the stickies. The better we coach the team towards self-reliance, the less up front we need to be. When they are ready, step back so they can grow.

> **Stepping Back**
>
> A manager once told me that as a Scrum Master my goal should be to work myself out of a job. To coach the team to the point that they no longer need a Scrum Master. This is an awesome goal that you should strive for as well. You will never be able to reach it, but you should constantly strive for it.
>
> What you will find is that as you coach the team to be stronger, there is always another level that they will need coaching on. They always have mental boxes that need to be opened and expanded. I often say that if the Scrum Master has been doing their job correctly in coaching the team, then from an outside perspective it looks like they are not doing anything. In reality, they are saying only what is needed, when it is needed, in order to keep the team moving forward.

This can seem overwhelming to have to do this much preparation for a meeting that happens every couple of weeks. Your teams will know if you are just going through the motions or truly looking out for them. Earn their trust, do the work and help them succeed. Now that you have prepared yourself for the meeting, it is time to prepare the room.

Prepare the room for the event

Depending on the retrospective game and approach you have chosen you will need to setup the room differently. If you are using small and large stickies, make sure you have plenty, as well as plenty of markers and/or pens. If you are doing a game like *Flying a Kite* then bringing in a physical kite makes the game come alive more for the team. Anything you can do to help focus the team and show them you are willing to go the extra mile for them will strengthen your relationship with them, making your job easier when you need to have the difficult conversations. There will always be difficult conversations over the course of time, but these tend to lead to the greatest advancements.

If you are doing this virtually, you will likely need to plan ahead to setup the meeting in such a way to allow the team to interact with a virtual board that you setup for the game you are playing. You can also take advantage of break out rooms to encourage individual engagement for the meeting. Many of these structures require setup before the team gets into the meeting as you want the facilitation to look seamless and polished.

Run the meeting

When you start the meeting, it is important to take the time to explain the retrospective game that you will be playing with the team. This is especially important if you are introducing a new game to the team. Make sure they understand the categories and then open the space for them to start the conversation.

Comfortable in Uncomfortable Silence

In most facilitations, especially retrospectives, you need to be comfortable letting silence hang in the air. Don't attempt to fill it right away. Most people have a hard time staying in silence and will speak up in order to fill the silence. Since we are attempting to get the team engaged, this technique will help draw them out.

For most new facilitators this is one of the toughest things to do. Whenever you ask a question, you will need to do this as well. You need to wait at least seven seconds for people to reply. They need to hear the question, process it to come up with an answer or question, and then take a couple seconds to get ready to speak up. Although difficult, this is an incredibly important skill to get good at as a Scrum Master.

Depending on your team, you may need to gently prompt and encourage the team to speak up. You can do this by asking probing, open ended questions of the team to get them to think about how they are working instead of just the work they do. This is when you can use your knowledge of observing the team to help you come up with the right questions to guide them to their own conclusions and improvement initiatives.

> **Agile Coaching Principle**
> "That's the way we have always done it" is the most dangerous phrase in the English language
>
> Challenge the status quo. There are always improvements to be made. This line of thinking stifles creativity and innovation. It also decreases the sense of empowerment for the team, leaving them deflated and demoralized.

You will need to challenge them to think differently than what they are used to. If they tell you that there is nothing that can be done to fix something, ask them to tell you how they would fix it if they could. If we allow ourselves to believe the status quo is the only way, we deny ourselves any chance to get real improvements.

When there is a natural lull in the conversation, you can kick start it again by sharing your observations with the team. When you are finished sharing each observation, ask them what they think about that? Have they observed the same thing? Do they think it is an issue? This is generally enough for most teams to get people attempting to problem solve. If the team rejects the observations, don't defend them, let them drop. Generally, this is the case when the team is not ready to address that issue. Move on and keep it on your list for another time. Let them work on something they are ready to tackle.

> **Coach the team for where they are**
>
> Many Scrum Masters run into issues when they start to coach the team to where they, the Scrum Master, feel the team should be. When working with individuals and teams, you need to constantly assess where they are on the Agile learning curve and coach them for this location. You will generally get a feel if your assessment is on target based on their response. If you shot too low, they will feel you are patronizing them, if you shot too high, they won't be able to

> follow. Look for the body language signals to know if you hit your mark and adjust as needed.

It is easy for the team to fall into the trap of using the retrospective as a venting session. You will need to monitor this. If the opinion being voiced is truly something out of the control and scope of the team, you can ask how that relates to the team and the work they produce. Let them talk about anything they wish, but don't let them dwell on things outside the team's control or influence. Things within their control and influence can be talked about to drive towards actions that the team can take. You will also need to make sure the conversation stays at a constructive level. This does not mean to attempt to avoid conflict, the team needs conflict to function fully. However, the conflict must remain constructive with mutual respect and not devolve into destructive conflict like shouting and name calling. We are all professionals trying to work together. Argue the ideas, not the people. Anything that the team identifies as something they are unhappy with or is an obstacle should result in an action that can be taken. Most times the action is something the team can do other times it might be for someone on the team to have a conversation to attempt to influence the change. If the retrospective ends without at least one action item, then it is likely you did not drive hard enough for them to come to actionable steps. Learn from this experience and try again next time. No matter how good the sprint went, there should always be at least one thing the team can work on to attempt to make an improvement.

Agile Coaching Principle
Continuous Improvement

Never accept things as they are, there are always things we can do to make our work environment better. Look for it. Take the time to inspect and adapt to make things better.

Every action item should have a single owner. Teams will be tempted to say the team owns some items. I have found that when everyone owns an item, no one does as everyone thinks someone else will do it. Make sure the team knows that owning an item does not mean they have to do all the work. When someone agrees to own an item, they are agreeing to hold the team accountable on completing it. You may be tempted to take ownership of many of these items. However, if you do you will be responsible for holding the team accountable for some of these. It is better to resist the urge to jump in and save them and let them own it. After all, if no one cares enough to own it, they are unlikely to follow through with it. Another thing is that no action item should be assigned to someone who is not present in the room during the discussion. If someone else needs to do the work, then change the action item to be for someone to follow up with them and request the work to be done. The action item should also be clear enough and small enough to be able to be completed within a single sprint.

As the team members share their thoughts and ideas it is important for you to ask clarifying questions to ensure that everyone is having the same understanding of what is being said. Just because something makes sense to you does not mean it makes sense to everyone else. A good technique for this is active listening. When the statement is said, put it in your own words and ask it back. You could say, "I think I heard you say…was that correct?" This not only clarifies what they were saying, but it also lets them know you were listening, really listening to them. Hint, this is a great way to build trust with the team and demonstrate that you are the Scrum Master they want.

Closing the meeting

Eventually the time comes to end the meeting. This could be because you run out of the time-box for the meeting, or because the team is done. In the beginning, it may be difficult to know when they are truly done or just holding back. Experience is the key here; you will get it. Before letting everyone leave. Read back the action items that the team came up with. If there are too many, have them quickly vote on one to three to work on during the next sprint. The team will need to deliver important work from the backlog in the next sprint, so it is important to limit the number of improvements in a given sprint. Focus the list to the most important and make note of the rest. Ensure that all of the items chosen for the next sprint have a single owner. Confirm with that person that they accept owning the item. No one should be volunteered by someone else, also referred to as voluntold, to do something for the team.

If you have the time, another great idea is to go over any shout outs the team gave again. Ending the meeting by reminding people on how they appreciated each other is a great way to let them leave the meeting on a high note. This is a powerful tool to associate the retrospective with a meeting they enjoy and look forward to. Tell them you will correlate the notes and send them back out to them for any correction and/or clarification.

Follow up

As you told the team at the end of the meeting, type up anything that needs it. Once you complete it, send it back to the team for clarification. This also empowers them to keep the notes handy to remind them of any action items they agreed on. Once the team has confirmed the notes, you will be able to add the action items to the backlog, especially the ones that the team agreed to do in the next sprint. These need to get move to the top to be brought into the sprint during planning. This prioritization is allowed as the team agreed to the work, and we need to make sure we are constantly improving our work so we can deliver more in the future.

Research Retrospective Games

Engaged teams with three variations of retrospective games

As I stated in the previous chapter, the retrospective event is critical for a Scrum Master to get right. How well you facilitate this meeting can make or break your relationship with your team, so it important to ensure they stay encouraged, engaged, and empowered in every retrospective that they go to. Since it is so important to keep teams engaged in a meeting that happens as frequently as the sprint retrospective, you will need more than one way to run this meeting.

If you google *Agile Retrospective Games* you will find a ton of games than you could run with your teams. Note that not all of them are worth running, so filter accordingly. I have discussed the parts that should be present in all flavors that you run in the previous chapter. We will now go into more detail on three different games you can use for your retrospectives to fill out your initial tool belt. With these four, *New Box* from Chapter Three and the three from this chapter, you should have a good foundation for these meetings and hopefully you will be encouraged to go out and find more.

Facilitate SaMoLo

This is one of my standby retrospective games. It is straight forward and an easy one to introduce new people to when they are learning what a retrospective should be. There are many games that are just different flavors of this one with different names. Some examples of others that are very similar are: *Plus-Minus-Delta, Start-Stop-Continue,* and *Starfish*. So, by learning this one you are actually getting familiar with a general range of games that are done in much the same way.

SaMoLo stands for Same As, More Of, and Less Of. As long as you memorize that, then you know the categories the game uses. Besides being my go-to game, this is probably the easiest one I know. In the previous chapter, I talked how you can use different approaches to any game, such as having the team call out ideas or have them write ideas down on stickies. Although I will use one approach in this break down, you can apply any approach that seems fitting.

Setup for this game is fairly simple. Put up four large stickies and label each one of the first three with one of the categories for the game. The fourth will be for any action items the team comes up with. After you explain what the categories are and remind them how retrospectives work, encourage them to start calling out ideas. Record each idea in the correct category. If you need to paraphrase or ask clarifying questions make sure that what you accurately summarize the ideas from the team. You do not need to record the entire conversation, but you should make note of enough to remind the team of the conversation they had. If the idea mentioned is in the more of or less of categories, ask the team what they feel they could do to achieve the desired idea. Record these on the action item sticky.

It is important to note that there are two schools of thought on driving straight to action items. One is that to maintain the flow of consciousness you should just record the ideas. Once the ideas begin to slow down, then you can go back over each to find action items for them. I am a believer in the second school of thought which is to drive to action right away. The reason I believe this is a better approach is that generally when an idea is added to the board there is a discussion that accompanies it. If you do not take the opportunity to drive that conversation to an action right away then when you come back later to do it, the team tends to repeat the conversation again. To me this is not an efficient use of the team's time. Of course, I could be wrong, which is why I am including both ideas here so you can choose which works best for you and the team.

At this point, do not worry about the number of action items you acquire. Keep the team talking and driving to possible action. Remember to have a name responsible for owning each one as well. The reason to not stop after you have a couple is you never know which of the mix the team thinks are the most important to address. Once all the ideas have been discussed and driven to action, then you can evaluate with the team. If you have more than three action items, you can suggest to the team to only take on the most important ones, and leave the rest for a future date. They might take your suggestion or they might not. If they do, you can do a round of dot voting to determine the highest priority items for them to agree to complete in the next sprint. If they choose to keep all of them, you might want to double check that one person does not own a bunch of items as this will likely decrease the chances that everything will get done. Also, make sure you are not just taking all of them, the team needs to own their own improvements if they are to become self-reliant.

Al Kraus

Facilitate Learning Matrix

My experience with learning about the *Learning Matrix* game is an example of our entire learning curve. When I first read the write-up, I wanted to run it. After that first time running it, I knew two things. First was how much I like the game. It is sometimes easier for people to put thoughts into the aspect of happy with and unhappy with than the categories used for *SaMoLo*. Second, was that I loved the idea of a Shout Outs section in the game. Once I finished that first time, I knew I would add a Shout Outs section to any game I ran from that point on. As an example, *SaMoLo* became *SaMoLo+*, which is how I recognized that I had added something to the base game.

In addition, I have found that when I have to facilitate a large retrospective, like a release retrospective, this is a really good game to use. These bigger facilitations normally cover a much longer period of time, and as such, the increased ease of remembering what made us happy or unhappy draws more out from the large crowd. It also helps having the shout outs for people that went above and beyond to help throughout the release.

You can also have a little fun with this one. Instead of just writing the categories up on the top of the stickies, you can draw icons to represent them. Even if you believe you cannot draw, trust me you can, but that is a different conversation, draw them anyway. People will be able to understand what they are.

To setup to run this game, put up four stickies and label/draw icons for the categories. The categories are:

- ➢ Things people are happy with (Smiley Face)
- ➢ Things people are unhappy with (Frowny Face)
- ➢ Ideas for improvement (Lightbulb)
- ➢ Shout Outs (Megaphone or Bouquet of flowers)

The happy with and unhappy with categories are fairly self-explanatory. Shout outs, as I talked about are for people to recognize someone else for what they have done. For example, "I want to give a shout out to Mary for automating our test cases; it saves a lot of time as we commit code." The only category that needs a little more discussion is the Ideas for Improvement. As you would expect, this is where you add your action items. But you can also add general ideas that the team comes up with. Ideas that they may need to percolate for a while before they take action on. This can be extremely useful to help break a team out of any mental rut that they find themselves in.

I have also found that you can use this retrospective game as a quick litmus test to see where the team is mentality. Generally speaking, if the team has more items in shout outs than unhappy with, they are in a good place. If there is a good deal of items in unhappy with as well as shout outs, then the team is likely succumbing to release pressure and having to work extra to meet an approaching deadline. If the team has a lot of items in unhappy with and little to none in the shout outs, then they are extremely low on morale and you should be looking for ways to bring them back together and to have more fun together. Take them to lunch at least.

Facilitate Sailboat

Retrospective games do not always have to follow the same patterns. Sailboat is a good example of how you can use imagery to change how people are thinking about the conversation. When you change the way they view their work, they are often surprised by what they discover. For example, I was working with a team and used this approach. The team came to a huge Ah ha moment. They realized that at that time the biggest thing holding them back was their engineering manager. Let me tell you, that lead to some difficult conversations. It also led to the team taking a giant leap forward on their Agile maturity curve as well.

Sailboat is setup fundamentally different than the previous two examples. That said, there are other retrospective games that are done similar to this one. *Force Field* is a good example that also uses this type of imagery to get the team to think differently about their environment. Sailboat is easier to do on a big dry erase board but can be modified to work with stickies as well. Generally, I start by drawing a sailboat on the board. This is placed towards the right edge and fairly high up on the board. You will want plenty of space to write to the left of and beneath the boat. In full disclosure, I am right-handed so I think this way, there is nothing saying that putting the sailboat on the left side does not work. Decide which way is more comfortable for you and run with it. You will also want to setup a stickie for any action items that come out of the conversation.

Once the team has gathered you will need to introduce the game to them. First, have the team image themselves as a sailboat floating on the water. If you have the time and the team agrees, this might be a good spot for guided meditation. That of course is strictly optional. With the team picturing themselves as the boat, ask them what is helping them move faster and achieve more. List these ideas as winds blowing into the sails of the ship. Then ask them, what is holding them back from going as fast or as far as they could go. Add these items below the water line behind the boat. Once you do, draw a line from them to the boat. These are the anchors the team is dragging behind them. Continue to record the ideas as the team identifies them.

Once the ideas start to slow down, you can ask the team which they think would have the greatest impact on getting the sailboat to go faster. Increasing the winds blowing in the sails? Or cutting loose some of the anchors being dragged behind them? Generally speaking, it is more helpful to remove anchors than increase the winds but let them decide for themselves. Assuming they decide on cutting the anchors loose, ask them which of the identified anchors do they think is the biggest. This could be done with a round of dot voting, or just by conversation. If they do choose the winds, follow the same process to drive towards action. Then ask them what it would take to cut that rope and lose the anchor. Drive this conversation to action. Often there may be many actions that would be required to cut the rope. Have the team decide which they think are doable within the next sprint and get someone to own making sure that it is done.

In addition to the retrospective itself, if you have a way of keeping the information around, you can periodically pull it back out and ask the team if they have identified any more winds or anchors, and if they have cut any more ropes. By doing this, the team can more easily see the progress they are making. Over time there should be fewer anchors and more winds as they continue to figure out ways to cut additional ropes.

Distinguish Between Popular Frameworks

Choose the best approach for your teams

You may or may not know already, but the Agile mindset and the Scrum best practices are a balance of ideas between common sense and being counter-intuitive. In many ways, the best practices are simple to understand, however they are difficult to implement and maintain. As the Scrum Master for your team, it will be imperative for you to know these processes and best practices so that you can help guide your team not only on how to use them, but how to stay with them through times of stress. One difficulty in attempting to simulate the Scrum processes is that most simulations are missing the mess and the deadline pressure of real life. It is fairly easy to be dedicated to the rules of the game during a simulation; it is much harder to do when pressure is applied at your real job. In order to best support our teams, we need to make sure that we have a firm understanding of the frameworks and best practices in our tool belts so we can use the right tool at the right time.

Explain Scrum framework

> *"When mores are sufficient, laws are unnecessary; when mores are insufficient, laws are unenforceable."*
> ~ *Émile Durkheim*

Frameworks, like Scrum, are very similar to this point of view. We use the structure of the framework to allow the team to build their Agile muscle. As that muscle becomes stronger, we need to rely on the framework less and allow them to customize their processes to best suit them. This is also described by the concept of Shu Ha Ri.

Shu Ha Ri

Shu Ha Ri is a Japanese idea explaining the progress that anyone or team goes through while mastering a new skill or process.

Shu – This is the stage when you are first learning. During this stage it is recommended that you follow the processes as described and concentrate on the "doing". Learning why the best practices were developed, building on successes, and experimenting. This is when teams work on setting up their foundation and aligning their environment to better support the team.

Ha – At this stage, the team has gotten the foundations of the processes down and established a supportive environment. This is when they can begin to expand their experimentation to bigger ideas. This is made possible because of the foundational work they put into place during the Shu stage. With the increased understanding of the underlying values and principles, teams in Ha can begin to bend the rules of the processes to better suit themselves.

Ri – This is the most evolved stage. Once a team has come to embody the values and principles, they can ascend them and find new and innovative ways of putting them into practice. The team begins to "Be" these new beliefs and values and no longer thinks of just the "doing". This higher state allows them to better adapt to their specific situations.

Part of our job is to help the team figure out which stage they are truly in and then adjust our coaching based on that location. In order to do this well, we need to have a firm grasp of the framework and how it is used to deliver value.

Scrum Values

Within the Scrum Guide are listed five core values. These are listed because without them, you cannot successfully implement Scrum in anything other than in name only. When implemented correctly working on a Scrum team can be an engaging and fulfilling experience. However, when working on a team that is doing Scrum in name only, it tends to be frustrating and demotivating. We must keep these Scrum values in mind and do everything we can to help foster them amongst our teams. Each of these values can be demonstrated many different ways within the team construct. We will just provide a few, but while you are observing your teams see how many of these you can find in their interactions.

Courage

There are so many ways to see why courage is important to an Agile implementation and to the Scrum framework. It takes courage to speak up about things that are not going well. It takes courage to accept the responsibility of empowerment. And let us not forget, it takes courage to say "No". In the absence of courage, you have fear. Fear of admitting to mistakes, fear of speaking up that you might receive retribution from managers, or complete lack of empowerment to make decisions. In a culture like this, no one wants to take the responsibility for a decision and they waste a lot of time running around making sure that everyone is in agreement before moving forward.

Focus

Straight from the Agile tenets I talked about before, focus allows us to be more productive. By reducing our amount of context switching we can maximize our productivity. Think about your normal work day. How much time during the average hour of work do you think you get of focused, productive work? Keep in mind time checking email, getting coffee, talking in the hallway and surfing the net do not count towards this "productive" time. Most people admit that it is likely about half an hour of productive work for every hour in the office. There is a technique you can use called ten and two. The way it works is that you set a timer for ten minutes. For that time, you focus solely on work without doing anything else. At the end of the ten minutes, you give yourself two minutes to do anything else, like get coffee, check email, or look something up online. It sounds a little strange I know, but if you do the math, using this technique would keep you focused and productive for fifty minutes every hour. How much more productive do you think you could be if you could stay this focused all day?

Openness

True openness cannot exist without courage. However, even if you are courageous it does not mean you are open. We need to be open to new ideas and ways of doing things. Open to learning new skills in order to be a team player. Open to being challenged on our designs and thoughts in order to collaborate and reach an even better design. Again, think about what a culture might be without this. How productive do you think we would all be if no one was open to listen to the ideas of others?

Respect

I cannot envision a team coming together and actually functioning as a team if the members do not have respect for each other. However, it is not enough just to say that we respect each other. We have to show respect in how we act and treat each other. Being on time for meetings can be seen as a sign of respect, likewise not interrupting someone while they are talking. Another form of showing respect as a Scrum Master is staying out of the team's solution space. In addition to these ideas, there are lots of other little ways to show respect and as Scrum Masters we need to learn our teams well enough to know how they see respect so we can ensure that we follow through in those ways. What do you think an environment without respect would look like? Would you want to work in a culture like that?

Commitment

There is an old saying, "Say what you will do, and do what you say." The value of commitment is the embodiment of this phrase. We need to be accepting when teams have difficulty completing everything by the forecasted time, as there is always learning opportunities. That said, we should be able to expect that teams routinely deliver between eighty to a hundred and twenty percent of what they forecast that they can deliver. Roadmaps and release plan need to be adjusted as more information is made available, but no one should feel that the team is not committed to delivering the highest value for the customer. What do you think a culture where no one follows through on their commitments would be like? Do you always deliver on your commitments?

Scrum Defined

Before we jump fully into defining Scrum, let's start with talking about the difference between a methodology and a framework. A methodology is a set of standardized processes and methods that produce predictable results. A framework is a supporting structure built around guidelines and values. So why is this distinction important? Because although Scrum has processes and procedures designed to manage the work to be done, it purposely does not contain detailed directions on how the work should be done; this is in order to allow teams the freedom to discover their own ways of working that work best for them. There are recommended best practices that can be used with the framework, but most of these come from Extreme Programming which is a very technical software development Agile methodology. It is this very supporting structure that allows Scrum to be used by any type of team including those outside of software development. It also allows teams the room to customize the framework to best suit their needs. So, we know that Scrum is a framework, but what else is it? Scrum is an Agile delivery framework that allows for managing the delivery of any kind of product or service. It is important to understand that Scrum will not fix your problems. It makes your problems visible so that you can fix them. We will cover more of the details of the structure of Scrum later in this chapter.

Important Note

Scrum will not fix your problems. It makes your problems visible so that you can fix them.

Contrast with Traditional Approach

With traditional project management, we approach a problem with the assumption that we can do enough analysis and research to understand everything that needs to be contained within the solution. With the list of everything we want to include in the solution, we come up with a detailed plan on when the solution will be able be completed by. We design milestones using horizontal slicing in which we do all the analysis, then all the design, then development and finally testing before we roll our solution out to production and to our customers. This approach has been around for a long time as evidenced by how we naturally attempt to break our work down in this way. However, what we find is that most projects attempted this way tend to have several issues. One is that the projects tend to take longer than our plans for them which gives rise to the second problem, that they cost more than we initially thought they would. Worst is that in this day and age of fast moving and shifting customer needs, the solution we deliver does not meet the needs of the customers by the time we deliver it. It is this last issue, which lead a group of people who had been experimenting with new ways of working to gather at the Snowbird Ski Resort in Utah in 2001 where the Agile Manifesto was created.

For most of the complex projects that we work on in today's world, it is almost impossible to know exactly what you need as a solution in the beginning of the project. We need a way to quickly discover not just what the customer is asking for, but what they really need. We accomplish this though incremental and iterative development of the solution. This allows us to get feedback from the customers before we have built all the features and realign based on this feedback. So, instead of waiting for up to a year or more before finding out if what we are building will actually solve the customer's need, we start getting feedback by the end of the first sprint, and continue to get it every sprint after that. What we find is that we normally do not need to include every idea that we initially thought we would.

Explain Kanban principles

Some of you may have heard about another Agile approach called Kanban. Kanban uses lean principles to streamline the delivery of work and eliminate waste along the way. It implements the Agile tenets in a different way than Scrum. It is important that as

Scrum Masters we understand this approach as well, as there will be times that we can use some of its approaches in Scrum. Remembering that Scrum is a framework and not a methodology, when can use what is effective. An example of this would be to use lead time as a way of getting the team to see the importance of getting work to the verification as an even flow instead of all together at the end of the sprint.

In a lot of ways, Kanban can seem more intuitive than Scrum. However, it is important to keep in mind that Kanban does not have any of the guard rails that Scrum has so it can be much harder to have the discipline to use this framework effectively. Once the Agile mindset is completely embraced, Kanban can be a very powerful tool. Where Scrum is a better tool for product management to discover the best possible solution for our customers, Kanban is about streamlining a process. To this end, Kanban works extremely well for situations where you work in a repetitive manner. Examples of this are help desk support, production lines, and any other work that is more operational in nature where priorities change often enough that planning for any length of time is difficult.

Kanban works by using a visual board to track the work as it moves through the system. It allows you to see where work gets backed up and slowed down. This information allows the team to focus on those areas of constraints and to iterate on ways to increase the flow of work through the entire system. The concentration is on the flow of work through the system, because this flow of work is important to overall improvement. When we can increase the speed of an item through the system, we increase the system's ability to respond to changes. Like we talked about earlier, Kanban concentrates on making sure the work does not stay idle. This is why optimizing the flow of the whole system is more important than optimizing the productivity at one part of the system. It is a little counter-intuitive but sometimes optimizing a part of the system you can actually slow the entire system down.

It is important, and often done incorrectly, to setup the board correctly. The mistake most often made is that the board is created based on what the ideal flow of work should be. This becomes very hard to track the work as it actually happens and thus the board does not reflect reality and is of little use. The correct way to setup the board is to map the process as it is used today. There will be time enough to make changes to the system once we see what is actually happening as the work gets done.

Once the board is setup and in use with the system as it exists, you need to know how to use the board to point out issues. There are several ways the board can do this. These include Lead Time, Cycle Time, Work In Progress limits (WIPs), and thresholds. We will talk about all of these so that you understand how they can be used to identify where to focus for improvements. To help with the description, let us follow a team that is providing computer upgrades for their company. Their company has one thousand employees, and each of them needs to have their laptops upgraded to a new operating system. Currently the team works with twenty laptops in a batch and it takes ten days for each batch to be completed and returned to the employees. That means to upgrade all of the laptops for the company, it would take a little under two years (five hundred days). Let's call this team The Locos.

Lead Time is the time an individual item stays within the system. It measures the time from when the item enters the system to when it leaves it. For our example, it would measure from when the laptop was turned into the team until when the laptop is returned to the employee. As we always want to see improvement, our goal for the example is to decrease the Lead Time from ten days to five for the upgrade and setting up all new applications. As you can see by tracking the lead time, if we were to hit our goal, we would be able to decrease the time of the full upgrade from five hundred days to two hundred and fifty. This might not be the only way we can improve our process, but it is a good goal to start with.

The first step in our process improvements would be to determine which part of our process is eating up the most time. Lead time measures the complete time, but we need something a little more focused. Therefore, we will implement Cycle Time metrics. Cycle Time is how long an item stays within a subset of the system. By using this we can identify which parts of the system take the longest. For The Locos, we find that items tend to stay in the operating system imaging stage for an average of eight of the total ten days. This looks like a good place to start finding improvements.

The next tool we will employ is Work In Progress limits (WIPs). With this we limit how many items can be in the same state of the system at the same time. Currently, The Locos are working in batches of twenty laptops at the same time. This means that all twenty proceed to the operating system upgrade state at the same time, since we have identified this as a problem area, we need to take a closer look. When we do, we find that the upgrading of the operating system takes two days, but the team can only upgrade three machines at the same time. So, for most of the time, laptops are sitting idle waiting for their turn or waiting on the remaining laptops in the batch before proceeding. Since we know that we should be looking out for idle work, this appears to be a good place to start. Locos takes this into account and decreases their batch size to three. By doing this they move each batch to the next stage without waiting for all twenty to be done. This decreases the average cycle time for this stage to two days, but does add a waiting cue that holds the laptops until they are ready to be started. Even with these smaller batch sizes, the team start delivering laptops back to employees much sooner. The team decides to limit the number of laptops in the ready queue to just three, they soon get caught up and the colleagues start noticing a turnaround of four days. Wow, what an improvement. But we are not done yet.

The team is very happy with their success so far and is now driven to find even more improvements. They notice that occasionally a laptop gets held up in the application re-install stage. This is found to not be frequent enough to make adjustments to the WIP, so they decide to monitor it. They know a laptop should spend no more than one day here, but occasionally a laptop sometimes takes three days. They add a threshold of one day to the stage. A threshold is a time limit that an item should be in any stage of the system. If the threshold gets broken, immediate attention should be given to get things moving again. Shortly after, they notice the threshold gets broken by a laptop. The team investigates and finds that some of the laptops were not updated last time, so they have applications that do not need to be upgraded, they need to be replaced. The team uses this information to add a quick inspection stage before the application stage to determine if upgrades or replacements are needed. With that done, all laptops flow smoothly through the system.

In our example, The Locos were able to meet their goal as well as find additional improvements. In practice you might not see this much improvement this quickly, but when the guidelines and metrics are used correctly, you will be surprised how much you will get. There is another use for thresholds, and that is for helping to identify when the work needs to be broken down. Similar to the application of WIP in our example, items that wait too long to move may be too big to efficiently run through the system. By decreasing the threshold value on some stages, you can identify which they are and change your process to better suit your needs. Often the improvements that need to be made, in order for a batch size to be decreased, may take a good deal of innovation and time to put in place. The benefits gained will make this effort worthwhile in the long run.

Explain the importance of the Sprint

Have you ever tried to calculate how long it would take you to get somewhere by foot? This is relatively easy if things are consistent. If I know a person can run five miles per hour, and they need to go three miles, then it should take them about thirty-six minutes. However, if it is someone like me, I can run five miles per hour but only for short distances. Then I need to walk to catch my breath, or stretch out the cramp in my side, or maybe even sit and recover. With all that, it becomes much more difficult to estimate the time it will take, or even how much ground I can cover in any given time frame. When we take it that estimation is not a given, then we also have to look into something called the student syndrome. I'm sure you remember back in the day when you were given a month to write a research paper. Did you do a little work each day and steadily make progress on the report and turn it in early? Or did you do what most of us did in school, wait until the weekend before the paper was due and do it all at one time, staying up late if not all night in order to get the paper done on time. And knowing this, do you think you received the grade you could have it you had done it steadily throughout? This is student syndrome. We tend to take the time allotted for a task no matter how long the task actually takes.

You're probably asking yourself, okay so what does this have to do with sprints? With the introduction of the sprint, the work is broken down into quick bitesize deadlines with constant check-ins to mark the progress for the larger release. These quick deadlines provide a low dose of urgency to help keep everything moving towards delivery without allowing people to relax like they do when the deadline is far-off. Let me be clear, I am not insinuating that people are slackers or lazy, but rather it is human nature to relax until the deadline approaches, and then we stress and attempt to catch up. When we give in to this temptation, we run the risk of burning ourselves out. The sprint cycle evens this out so that we can continue at a higher rate delivery without burnout.

Scrum says that a sprint should be one to four weeks in length. So why not determine the length of the sprint based on the amount of work required to achieve the sprint goal. A team could decide the length of the sprint when they determine which stories they need for the goal. However, we have already talked about the need for predictability. If the sprint length varies, it not only makes it harder for the team to predict how much they can handle in the sprint, it also makes it harder to keep track of the release commitments. It also brings us back to estimating how long the work will take instead of using a more predictable method of story points per sprint. The main idea of the sprint is a regularly occurring timebox to allow for regular feedback for both the solution and the team. Once a sprint length is chosen it should stay consistent for as long as possible and should not fluctuate.

There are many reasons why the output of the sprint is important. First, it establishes a history of what the team can deliver. This historic record provides a baseline for release planning and helps to establish trust in those plans as the team delivers on them. It also provides for feedback on the solution so that plans can be adjusted as needed. The output of the sprint is also important to ensure that the process the team will use to do a release is exercised regularly so when the time comes to release, there is confidence that the process will go smoothly. In order for the team to have this confidence in the quality of the release, they must ensure that every story completed meets their Definition of Done. By ensuring everything meets this policy, the team can be sure that it is ready for release at any time. We will discuss the Definition of Done more in Chapter Eight.

Maintain Processes for Team

Coach your teams to increased creativity, empowerment, and productivity with the Scrum framework

Scrum is by far the most common Agile implementation approach. I believe that one of the reasons for this is because it is like Agile with training wheels. If you follow the roles, artifacts, and events as prescribed, you will start to see some benefits. This success then encourages more experimentation and improvements. Once you start getting this cycle of small successes, it becomes easier to embrace the mindset that drives the framework. In this chapter we will go into detail on the roles and artifacts described in the Scrum framework.

Describe Scrum roles

In Scrum, there are three roles defined. These are the Scrum Master, the Product Owner and the Team Members. Scrum does not have roles like Business Analyst, Developer, Tester, or Designer. That is not to say that those skill sets are not important, but rather that it is all part of being a Team Member. In simple terms, the Product Owners is responsible for the vision, the "what" and "why" of the solution that is being built. The Team Members are responsible for the "how" the solution is built, this is why the team must be made up of people with all the skills required to deliver the solution. Lastly, the Scrum Master is responsible for the process used by the Product Owner and Team Members in order create the solution.

If you talk to Scrum purist, Scrum Master is a role and not a position. The idea being that anyone on the team should be able to take up the role and assist the team forward. I agree that on an extremely Agile mature team this might be the case, but most teams are not there yet. I have been in this role as a developer/Scrum Master. It was a time period that I felt extremely unproductive and not providing value at all. Whenever I spent time on the Scrum Master part, I was stealing time from the development work; when I worked on the development, I could not stay heads up to help the team. The effect that I saw for myself and confirmed by other in this position is that we kept the lights on. However, any improvements at the team level came slowly, if at all.

I once had a conversation about this with my manager at the time. I said, "I feel like I am shooting myself in the foot. I know that the Scrum Master work I am doing is the best thing I can do to help the team, but then I don't get time to improve my development skills. And at the end of the year, you are going to evaluate me based on how good a developer I am, not how good I am as a Scrum Master." His reply, "I had not thought of that. Yes, you are shooting yourself in the foot, but keep doing it, because that is what the team needs."

The position I was in is what I refer to as a hybrid role. This means that part of your time you are wearing one hat, and the rest another. We already talked earlier about the effect of context switching. When you are doing two roles like this you are always in a position of trying to balance the two, or more, roles. In addition, most people in the hybrid role actually prefer one role over the other. Like the situation with my boss that I described earlier, even if I was the best Scrum Master in the world, my evaluations would be done based on my skill as a developer which is what I went to school for and enjoyed very much. At the time I thought I was doing a good job as a Scrum Master, but once I was in a position to do the role full time, I learned a whole new level of what this role can do.

Like with most things, there are times when a hybrid role is not only acceptable, it is desirable. This is true when the team size is very small. Another time this can work well, like I mentioned earlier, is if the team is comprised completely by members that have completely adopted the Agile values and are functioning at an extremely high level of Agile maturity. This is the goal we should all strive to get our teams to. Another manager I worked for put it this way, "your goal as a Scrum Master is to try and work yourself out of a job." In my personal experience this is a very hard state to actually get to. Most teams can be coached to become extremely self-reliant, and yet they still benefit from having a Scrum Master. Agile and Scrum are simple, but not easy. And it is difficult for a team to stay focused on delivery and also drive towards process improvements for the team. It takes an extreme amount of discipline.

Scrum Master

The Scrum Master is responsible for helping drive improvements for a team. In order to do this, we help the team, and the organization, create an environment that allows the team to thrive and succeed. For me, there is little more fulfilling then seeing a team I have worked with shine like the sun and be recognized for their achievements. It is the fuel that drives me, and helps me to strive to improve every day in order to better help them. This environment consists of the team being empowered to create their own solutions, experiment with improvement ideas, and have a clear sense of purpose. I have heard it said that there are three main motivators for people. They are the drive for Mastery, Autonomy, and Purpose. When we can fulfill all three of these for our team, they ascend to another level of performance. In this context, mastery is the ability of the team members to increase their skill sets, not just in their specialty but also as a generalist within the team. Autonomy is the individual and the team's right to take the given vision and solve as they see fit to maximize value for the customer without someone looking over their shoulder and attempting to micromanage them. And purpose is the knowledge that what they are working on serves a higher value than just the piece they build, that it is part of something bigger.

Some of the main tools a Scrum Master uses are metrics. Metrics allow the team to gain insights on what they should focus on for improvements as well as to be able to see if their experiments actually improve their process. However, it is important to note that metrics can be a two-edged sword. It is vital to understand that we get what we measure. If we are not careful with which metric we decide to value, we can actually encourage the wrong behavior. For an example, let's see if we can increase the amount of value delivered to the customer. If our team can deliver a thousand points of value per sprint working just forty hours a week, our imaginary managers will deduce that if the team works fifty hours a week, they figure that the team should be able to deliver twelve hundred points of value. To this end, they decide to have the team members track how many hours they are at work with the incentives given if fifty hours a week is reached. Do you think the managers are going to get their twelve hundred points? Likely not, the metric just measures time so we can be assured that people will be "clocked" in for fifty hours. However, they are more likely to take coffee breaks or take a quick walk or otherwise be distracted. That is because what you are measuring and rewarding is time in the office. If the managers had been thinking of how to encourage the delivery of more value, then there needs to be a metric to measure the value delivered. This is typically done by the Product Owner assigning a business value to each story. This value would be separate from the estimated point value that the team assigns to the work. If they use a value delivered metric with an incentive if twelve hundred points of business value are delivered, do you think they will get it? Very likely. In addition, it is possible that the team might find a way to deliver this without the overtime. Obviously, this is a fictitious example, but this situation happens all the time. Make sure you are using the metrics that will support the behavior you are looking for.

Sometimes, a single metric will not give you the desired approach. For example, if you are using metrics for faster delivery, you will likely get faster delivery by the team taking short cuts in order to make the metrics. In this case, you will need a second metric to ensure that the quality does not go down as the team speeds up. Neither of these metrics alone would suffice but together than can be quite effective. Another thing to note about metrics is they should be used like red flags. They may indicate an issue but before you know for certain, you need to observe and have conversations to see if the reason that a metric was off is a real issue or not.

There are some common metrics and I am going to cover some of those. If the team decides on a behavior to track not covered by these, you can create any way of measuring it with the team, just keep in mind how the metric could be gamed. Some of the metrics discussed come from a white paper by Scott Downey and Jeff Sutherland titled "Scrum Metrics for Hyperproductive Teams: How They Fly like Fighter Aircraft".

Velocity

Velocity is the measure of how many points of work the team has delivered each sprint. It is a simple calculation as you total all points of stories that are completed in the sprint. Stories that are not completed are sent back to the backlog or carried forward. We discussed carryover when talking about facilitating the planning meeting. When being used for sprint planning, we generally use the average velocity of the past three sprints. This allows for changes in the team to be incorporated quickly so the team can adapt their plans. Velocity is also used in release planning. When used this way, we use the average of the past eight sprints. We use the past eight sprints to have a more consistent velocity. To calculate the estimated number of sprints a release will take, you take the total estimated points for the release and divide by the average velocity. We will go into more depth on release planning in Chapter Nine. It is important to note that each team will have its own scale and you cannot compare velocity across teams.

Accuracy of Forecast

Accuracy of forecast is a measure how well the team delivers on the stories they committed to in planning. The calculation is to divide the number of points completed by the number of points planned. The goal for this metric is to keep the average score between eighty and a hundred twenty percent. When used correctly, this metric allows the business to gain trust in the release plans and road maps that the team has committed to. Because this metric is a ratio, it can be used to compare teams.

Estimation Accuracy

Estimation accuracy is a measure of how well the team is estimating the work. This is normally tracked at the task level and compares the estimated hours and actual hours on the tasks. Similar to accuracy of forecast, this is calculated by actual hours for the task divided by the estimated hours on the task. Since the estimated hours are used during planning as a sanity check on the velocity planning, having good estimation is important for the team. We discussed this type of sanity check in Chapter Two. Again, since this is a ratio you can compare this metric across teams.

Work Capacity

This is a metric to be a little careful with, but it is useful in some of the other metrics listed in coming sections. This is simply the total number of team member hours available for the sprint. There is a slight difference of opinion on how many hours a day you should count in this metric. As most people work eight hours a day, one school of thought is this is the number you use. My opinion is to use six hours a day as this takes into account that everyone will lose some time, walking between meetings, checking emails, getting coffee and such. Make sure to account for anyone that is only partially on the team that they are not counted for the full time. Since this is calendar time you could compare this across teams; however, I don't see a lot of value in doing so.

Focus Factor

This is a good metric to indicate how much of the team's time is actually going towards the work of the sprint. You calculate the focus factor by dividing the total actual time recorded on the tasks by the work capacity. Using this metric, the team can see how much time they are losing to work they are doing off the sprint board. Often this is because the managers of team members are giving them work to do that the team is not aware of. Once more, being a ratio, this metric can also be compared across teams.

Impediments

Another key duty of the Scrum Master is to help the team remove impediments. In this context, an impediment is anything that prevents or slows the teams and their ability to deliver value. It is important to remember, like in the oath when you enlist, that you need to protect "against all enemies, foreign and domestic". What I mean by this is some impediments will be from outside team, but sometimes you need to point out that the team is holding themselves back. When a team first starts working in an Agile way, the external impediments are very easy to spot, but as we work to remove them, we tend to find more and more often the impediments are within the control of the team. Often these internal impediments are hard to spot so you will need to share your observations until the team can see the issues and then address them.

Whenever the impediment is within the team's control it is a straight forward path to resolving it once the team decides to. Some impediments the team will need your help with. When the team cannot solve the issue themselves and you can help, do what you can to help them out. Other times you will need to escalate the concerns to those that can do something about it. As your team matures on their Agile journey, there should be less that they cannot do on their own, but when they do help them to solve and learn how to handle it if it arises again.

Product Owner

The Product Owner is the voice of the customer for the team. They not only need to understand the domain that the team will build a solution for, they also need to know how to interview and otherwise get the customer's wants and needs. There are a lot of tools and techniques that Product Owner can use in order to gain this empathy. Two common tools used for this purpose are personas and journey maps.

Personas are a fictitious representation of a customer. They are used to represent a segment of the customer base and make it easier for the Product Owner and team to empathize with their situation. They give a face and a name to the customer. They make the customer come alive while the team builds the solution for them. The better acquainted the team gets with the personas the more they strive to help them. For any given product or service there will likely be many different personas. Each persona will have a slightly different experience with your solutions.

A journey map is a description of how one of the personas experience your product or service. For each step in the journey, we record how the customer feels, what they might be thinking, and make special note of any pain and pleasure points they may have. By filling out the journey we get a much better idea of what would make the customer happy and how we can exceed their expectations.

The team is responsible for creating a high-quality solution for the customer, but it is the Product Owner that determines what the team should build and explains why the customer wants it. This starts with the personas and the journey maps. A pain or pleasure point is identified and then possible solutions are ideated for it. These ideas are then added to the product backlog as large and likely vague ideas. Once there, the Product Owner will be responsible for prioritizing the items with the most valuable on top. There is normally a hierarchy to items on the product backlog and different companies will use different names for levels in their hierarchy. This is one scheme that can be used. I will call the initial large items Themes. The Product Owner can then start working with the team in order to break down the theme into epics and then into stories that can be refined and eventually brought into a sprint.

There are many techniques that a Product Owner can use to prioritize the backlog. We will talk about four different techniques that can be used in a little bit but we should not discount a Product Owner's gut feeling for which story or epic should be moved to the top. As the Product Owner becomes more in tuned with the customers, they can develop instincts on what will help them. These of course should be tried and tested quickly to see if the instinct was right.

Weighted Shortest Job First

In this approach, each item is given an index based on the cost of delay and the estimated duration the item will take to build. Each item is given a cost associated based on how much we would lose for delaying the release of this item. This takes a good deal of information about the market and customer needs and is normally assigned by the Product Owner. The next thing is an estimate of how long the item would take to implement. This estimate is normally done by either the team or a review board of experts. With these two numbers you take the cost of delay and divide by the duration. You can then prioritize the items with the highest index first.

MoSCoW

MoSCow is an acronym to help you memorize the four categories used in this method. They are Must Have, Should Have, Could Have, and Won't Have. This approach will not give you a single column priority like the other methods but it will help in the grouping of items to help define a Minimum Viable Product (MVP). We will go into more depth on the MVP shortly when we talk more about the backlog. It also makes the finer grained priority easier as you only have to prioritize the item with one of the sections, normally just the must have items. This process could be done by just the Product Owner or along with the team as well. Each item is assigned to a category based on its importance to delivering the highest value to the customer. Must have items are the table stakes required for the solution to be considered viable. Items are put into the should have category if they are not table stakes, but really should be included. Could have items are the ones that if we have time, we could include these items. Won't have items are the ones that at this time we feel are not valuable enough to justify the cost of building the solution. We want to keep these around to see if our information changes later on. Once the items are separated, then each category could be prioritized to create a single ranked backlog.

Value-Ease

This is a very fast approach using the dot voting technique. First calculate the number of votes for each person per the instructions in Chapter One. Then you do two rounds of voting. The first is for everyone to place their votes on what they think are the highest valued items in the list. The second round, the team votes on which items they feel would be the easiest to implement. Each item can then be ordered based on the value and ease of implementation with items with the highest value and ease at the top of the list.

Highest Risk

With this approach each item is assigned a value by how much risk is involved in the implementation. The items are ordered with the riskiest on top so that risks can be mitigated as quickly as possible. This can be used as a good approach along with MoSCoW.

Backlog Maintenance

Once the backlog is setup it is not set in stone. The Product Owner should be updating it with new items, removing outdated or unneeded items, and reprioritizing based on additional information. This information can come from the team making progress on the backlog or from additional interactions from customers. This is especially the case once a first pass of the solution is ready to be tried and tested with customers to gain their insights on how the solution should be improved.

Once created, the backlog should be visible to everyone so that people know how the initiative is going. They can also add information to the backlog by working with the Product Owner to help refine the backlog or prioritize items to better help our customers. It is important that the backlog is maintained in priority order at all times. It is also important that the top of the backlog, the work soon to be worked on by the team, should be refined and ready to be started. We talked about refinement in Chapter Two.

Product Owner Issues

There are a couple of situations that are sometimes implemented that can cause issues with the team's ability to deliver value effectively. You need to be on the lookout for these and then work with the Product Owners and the organization to try to resolve them.

Multiple Product Owners

There are times when the organization decides that more than one person should own the solution to be created. There are many reasons they chose this path. One reason is the thought that one person should speak for the business and the other should speak for the technical implementation of the solution. In my opinion this comes mostly from a lack of trust that the team can design and implement the solution from a technical aspect. The concern with this approach is that it is very hard to lead by committee, even a committee of two. Both people will likely have different opinions on how the backlog should be prioritized and will likely give conflicting direction to the team. The team can also begin to feel disempowered as they feel they need agreement from both parties before a decision can be made. This, of course, is in addition to likely having to ensure all technical decisions goes through the technical Product owner.

Product Owner by Proxy

Another common issue is the Product Owner by proxy. This happens when the organization decides on a Product Owner that does not have the time to work with the team. So, a decision is made to have someone "fill in" for the Product Owner when interacting with the team and in all of the Scrum meetings. The problem is that the proxy has no authority to make decision about the solution. Which means whenever the team needs a question answered the proxy needs to find time with the empowered Product Owner and interpret for the team. This can lead to massive delays as well as miscommunications and mistakes. The person chosen for the Product Owner position needs to have the time to work with the team daily in order to increase delivery speed and reduce mistakes.

The Absent Product Owner

The other common issue with a Product Owner, is when they are too busy and don't show up. The team is left with little to no direction and no ability to ask questions for clarity. Not only does this lead to delays, but it also leads to a large amount of rework as the team makes assumptions in attempts to keep the work moving, only to later find out that their assumptions do no match the Product Owners expectations.

Team Member

As important as the Scrum Master and Product Owner are, no solution would get built without the team members. Not only are they experts in their fields, they have to become experts at being on a team. The first step for the team members is to stop being a working group. They need to stop thinking of themselves as a group of individuals and start thinking of themselves as a team. No one on the team owns pieces of the work, the team owns it all. This shared ownership of the work is what will begin to bring them together. As they have conversations during refinement and planning, they will begin to learn about each other's skill set and understand why becoming cross-trained is vital to their predictability of delivery.

For the best possible outcome, they need to be empowered to organize themselves around the work. This is helped when the team remembers that Scrum is meant to be a game. They should view the daily stand up as a time to plan out the next move as a group for moving closer to their goal. Each action is a move in the game. And teams that work well together, win together.

Another characteristic of a winning team is that they are self-reliant. This is an extremely important point for the Scrum Master to understand. We need to help the team whenever we can, but we have to think long term. This is the process of stepping back we talked about. We need to get out of the team's way in order for them to hit their true potential. One of the misconceptions about the Scrum Master role is that she should act as a barrier to protect the team. What I can tell you is that if the Scrum Master tries to do this, people will find a way around them. They will call or email the team and still get them to do extra work. The best way for the Scrum Master to protect their team is to teach them that they need to protect themselves.

When I first tried telling my teams about this, I got a kick out of watching their eyes pop out of their heads at the suggestion. I would tell them, "I don't care who comes to you in the middle of the sprint, if it is someone from another team, your boss, or the CEO of the company. If they ask you to do work not in the sprint, your response should be something like 'I would love to, let me check with my team to see if it will interfere with our commitments'. If they insist, cave and do it, but let the Scrum Master know as soon as possible so they can follow up on it. I am not asking anyone to put their job in jeopardy, but as an Agile team this is part of your responsibility to help protect the team. More often than not what seems like a burning fire can wait until the next sprint." The team is only truly protected from outside noise when they act as the first line of defense and then use the Scrum Master to follow up and make sure the noise does not keep coming back. Besides the distraction from the sprint commitment, the other reason this is important is that work should flow to the team through the Product Owner. The reason for this is the Product Owner is communicating roadmaps and release plans to the business based on the team being dedicated to that work. Since they are responsible for setting the priority of the work, work flowing to the team from anyone else interferes with this priority. I have seen complete releases derailed because an engineering manager decided his people were needed on another project. In the end, it was the Product Owner, not the manager, that was held responsible for the missed deadline. If the Product Owner is to be held accountable for the priority of the work, they need to be given the authority to control that priority. It is up to the team to help defend that so that everyone delivers on their commitments.

Describe Scrum Artifacts

Whenever I hear the word Artifact, I cannot help but think of Indiana Jones, following clues to find hidden treasure. The Scrum artifacts are just as valuable. They help everyone stay on the same page, as well as to keep clarity and transparency. All of this helps to ensure that we are delivering the highest value at all times.

Product Backlog

We have talked about the product backlog before throughout the chapters so far. Now, let's dig down a little more and be more specific. We have already discussed that the product backlog contains all the possible ideas that can be included in a solution. It is possible and likely in some cases that to complete all of this work it could take years of effort. This is why the backlog must be kept prioritized so the highest value features can be completed and rolled out as quickly as possible in order to get more feedback on which of the remaining features are the most desired. This backlog will normally be broken up in some way. This could be by category, such as those used in MoSCoW or into a series of releases. The first release is normally referred to as a MVP. Minimum Viable Product (MVP) is the smallest set of features needed to be able to start to get actionable feedback from customers to ensure we are on the right track with our solution. It can be extremely difficult to pare down the list of possible features to this bare set. However, the better we do of pushing work into later releases the faster we can start getting the feedback we need.

One question that comes up often is how do we know if our backlog is healthy. There are several things that need to be in place for a backlog to be considered healthy. First, it needs to be well maintained. This means the Product Owner needs to be working in it regularly, adding and/or removing stories, adding details to the vision as well as prioritizing based on the latest information. This takes a good deal of time, and when you add in the time it takes to get the customer insights and feedback it becomes obvious why the Product Owner role needs to be dedicated to just providing this vision and perspective for the team. We have talked about how most of the backlog will be large placeholders so that ideas are not forgotten; only the top of the backlog is refined and ready to be started by the team. The question then becomes how much of the top of the backlog should be refined and ready. The best practice is to try to maintain about two sprints worth of backlog in a ready state. If you have less than this then the team runs the risk of not having enough work to fully plan a sprint. They also begin to lose a little bit of the next horizon thinking as everything seems to come up just in time or late. This lack of clarity can lead to misunderstanding and slow down delivery. On the other hand, if we have too much backlog in a ready state then the team has likely spent too much time in refinement working on stories and designs for things that could be deprioritized or need to be changed based on feedback. One team I worked with found themselves in the spot of having to scramble to refine stories for each sprint even though they had about eighteen months of backlog marked as ready. This was because almost all the stories they had sized were unimportant to the business at that time, and of the work the business wanted completed, they did not have enough to fill out a sprint. When you think about the amount of time that team spent refining the stories to have that much refined backlog, you can see how much time and resources were spent for work that might never see the light of day. Not to mention the delay to more valuable work that could have been delivered earlier. In point of fact, sometime later almost that entire backlog was thrown out and never used.

One more thing that we need to cover is what makes a well-defined backlog item. It is important to state again that the backlog items, whether epic, story or task, are just placeholders for conversations. That said there should be enough information on the item to reduce the chance for miscommunication. This does not mean that it needs to map out exactly how to implement the request, in fact it should not. It should clearly state the objective in terms of how it will help the customer and why the customer would want this change. It should also include how the Product Owner and the team will know when the item has been completed. There are a couple of best practices to help to ensure that backlog items are well written. The user story format from Mike Cohn is a great start. It uses a standard format and gives the critical information that an item should have. I first introduced this format in Chapter Two when we were talking about the sprint goal. For reference the format is:

As a <type of customer>, I want <some feature> so that <some reason>

This format allows the team to keep the customer in mind, as well as to know the reason for the request. This is critical, in that it allows the team to come up with additional ways that the reason could be addressed even if it is different than the original requested feature. The other important point is the acceptance criteria. This is how the team and Product Owner will know when the item is completed. There are two different approaches I will share with you. Both approaches work well when used, but different situations may lend toward one way or another. These approaches are:

Given <some condition> when <some action> then <some result>
And
Verify that <some action leads to some result>

The first format has additional benefits as if a story has several of these statements in the criteria, they could be used to help decompose the story into smaller stories. The additional benefit of the second format is that it lends itself well to how the item will be tested and verified by the team. Whichever format is chosen, every item should have clear acceptance criteria so that the conversations are as clear and concise as possible, which is the most important point of the item itself.

Sprint Backlog

The sprint backlog is pulled from the top part of the product backlog and is what the team has committed to try to get done by the end of the sprint. It is also the only part of the backlog that has been broken down into tasks and specific actions that the team needs to take. These tasks are the only time that items in any backlog are so specific that completing one does not in itself give value, as you need to complete all the tasks of a story in order for that item to be deliverable. This task level of detail is what allows the team to better support itself as they organize to get the work done. This is also the first time that items come out of a ready state and gets put into progress.

When talking about changing the sprint backlog throughout the sprint, the by the book answer is that no change should happen mid-sprint. Changes should wait until the next sprint planning takes place. However, what we see is that this is not always possible. So, the next question becomes who has authority to change the sprint backlog. The answer is the team, in negotiation with the Product Owner. The amount of change to the original backlog items determines the actions required to make adjustments. If the Product Owner needs to replace a story based on additional information on how to best deliver on the sprint goal, then the conversation is what and how much work may need to be pulled out of the sprint to make room for the new item to come into the sprint to better deliver on the sprint goal. The team should never just bring in the additional work without having a conversation if they still feel they can deliver all the original commitment as well as the additional work. There will also be times that the change is coming in because the sprint goal has changed. If this is just a clarification that indicates different stories are required then the team and Product Owner need to have a conversation on how to adjust to the new goal with minimum wasted effort.

There will occasionally be times where the majority or entire sprint backlog needs to be replaced. This can happen when a production issue or any other unforeseen situation comes up that requires the immediate attention of the team. In these circumstances, I recommend that the sprint be cancelled and the team immediately re-plans the sprint for the remaining time to best address the most important issues. Some organizations and culture look down on cancelling a sprint. However, I feel this is important as it sends a very clear statement that the team is adjusting to the business needs.

Let me tell you a story. I was working on a development team. Our team had a terrible reputation in the department for not being able to deliver on the items we committed to in planning. The reason for this was that within the first couple of days on any sprint we had a bunch of work dumped on the team that was always more important according to the Product Owner than the items we brought in during planning. We were not allowed to cancel the sprint, so by shifting focus to the critical things brought in, we did not have time to also finish the original stories. Our velocity was fairly consistent but it was not normally the original stories that got delivered each sprint. The reputation we received was because we could not signal that we were being responsive. The effects of this were lower morale on the team and lack of trust that the team could deliver on the road maps being communicated. This situation made us feel completely powerless and unappreciated. This is not a situation we ever want our teams to be in.

Sprint Burndown

The Sprint Burndown is a chart that shows the team the amount of work remaining in the sprint. This allows the team to see if they are on track to complete all the items or if they are behind or ahead. The chart shows the amount of work remaining in the sprint compared to an ideal line. The ideal line is calculated based on a consistent amount of work being completed each day to reach zero by the end of the sprint. This information can better help the team come up with their daily plans. If the team is ahead of schedule and feeling confident on the delivery of everything in the sprint they may decide to pull in additional work. This work is additional and not part of the sprint commitment. If the additional work gets completed, awesome celebrate with the team. But if we hold it against the team for not completing the additional work, we will only encourage them to not bring in additional work. This additional work can actually help the team discover their full velocity and should be encouraged as long as the work brought in during planning and the sprint goal can be completed. If the sprint burndown shows the team is behind, it can give a sense of urgency that helps them complete the work.

In order for the burndown to be an effective communication tool for the team, it requires that the backlog be kept up to date so that the burndown is as accurate as possible. If the information is not up to date, the team will lose confidence in the report. It is important for the Scrum Master to take steps to coach the team to hold itself accountable for keeping the sprint board and the burndown up to date.

There are two different ways that a team could use the burndown. This is to use story points or remaining hours. Depending on the team's preferences, use the type that will best help them. If the team brings in a lot of small stories then a story-based chart will work well for them. It will show how much of the work has been delivered and ready for the sprint review. However, if the team brings in larger stories that take more of the sprint to complete, than a story point-based chart will not give much detail as the only time it will change is when a story is completed. This is a good time for the remaining hour chart. By having the team re-estimate the amount of work remaining on each in progress task as they work, the team can see how much work is still needed to be completed to finish the sprint backlog. If the team is using all the metrics discussed earlier then this is relatively straight forward. It can be difficult to get the team members to re-estimate their tasks each day, but the effort pays off by the additional information in the burndown report.

Release Burn Up

The release burn-up is similar to the burndown chart and, in the beginning, they are often confused with each other because of the similar names. The burn-up chart displays information at a different level over a longer period of time. It normally covers the timeframe of an entire release or project. It will also have an ideal line based on a consistent rate of completed work in order to have all work completed by the due date for the release. At the top of the chart is the scope line. This line represents the estimated size of all work in the release. If features are added to the release this line will go up, if scope is removed in order to increase the chances of the date being hit, the line will go down. As the scope line changes, the ideal line is updated to show where the team should be. Another line is on the bottom of the chart which represents the amount of work in the release that the team has completed. Over time this line should rise up and met the scope line. Often when this chart is created, the completed line is extrapolated out to predict where this line and the scope line will meet. This informs the Product Owner if the release is on track to deliver on time and allows for better communication on the status of the release with the rest of the organization. Although, this report is typically updated by the digital tool being used as stories are closed. The Product Owner should ensure it is up to date after each sprint to facilitate those conversations. Keeping a chart like this updated, once the organization is trained on how to effectively use them, can eliminate the need for most of the status meetings that needed to occur during the traditional project management approaches.

Coach Your Teams to Improvement

Become the Scrum Master You Wish You Had

Every team deserves the type of coach that will push them enough to find improvement without pushing them too hard that they crumble from the pressure. It is easy to see this play out in sports, but with teams in the office it is not always that clear. When the Scrum Master does their job well, it is the team that typically gets the credit for the improvement. As I have mentioned before, our goal should be to set the team up so that they can shine like the sun. We have several tools to enable this. Using the Agile Tenets to break things down and drive improvement, helping the team remove impediments, and helping people understand how the traditional roles, like project manager, map to the new roles within Scrum are some the most powerful.

Identify how the Agile mindset drives improvement

The Agile Manifesto was signed in 2001 and documented the values and principles of the Agile mindset. Built upon this mindset have been many different implementations on how it can be used to improve delivery of customer focused solutions. In their simplest form, all of these implementations have four things in common. These are the four tenets of Agile. It is important as a Scrum Master to keep these in mind as they make a very powerful tool for teaching others how to begin to adapt to an Agile mindset, especially for people outside of the Information Technology disciplines. I have found it helpful to use this simpler approach to these concepts and have found that they resonate well with most people.

Visualize the Work

If we cannot find a way to visualize the work, then it becomes very difficult to identify what parts of a complex system we need to focus on to find improvements for the whole system. It becomes too easy for things to slip through the cracks, or for people to overly focus on their one piece of the system. This siloed focus can lead to over-optimization of a component which may actually slow down the system as a whole. There are many different ways that can be used to visualize the work. A simple to-do list is a limited form of visualization. Scrum uses the backlog and sprint board in order to visualize the state of the work in progress and encourage team collaboration in order to get it done. Kanban uses the Kanban board to visualize how the work progresses through the system. Regardless of how you chose to visualize the work, you will need to monitor the visualization in order to identify where the work gets hung up. By identifying the constraints of a system, we begin to understand what needs to happen in order to increase the delivery of the system.

Inspect and Adapt

The inspect and adapt cycle is critical for finding meaningful improvements to the flow of the system. We have a tendency to believe that we would naturally strive for continuous improvement every day. In fact, during a keynote in 2015, Mike Cohn explained that when he signed the Agile Manifesto, he did not believe that an Agile team should need to do a separate retrospective meeting because they should be innovating all the time. His catch-phrase from that speech was "I could be wrong". That keynote has stuck with me ever since. He goes on to say that now [then] that even on mature teams, we need to set time aside to innovate ideas for improvement. We all tend to get caught up in the daily grind of getting the work done to hit our deadlines. If we do not get in the habit of periodically pausing in order to reflect on how we are doing the work, we will continue to do things the way we have always done them. There is an old saying "If you always do what you always did, you'll always get what you always got". By pausing to reflect, we can adapt how we are working, identify impediments to remove, and vastly increase our ability to deliver value no matter what type of solution we are building. Most often this tenet is implemented by doing a regular retrospective as described in Chapter Three.

Limit Work in Progress

As counter intuitive as it may be, we find that when we limit our work in progress, we can deliver value more efficiently then when we attempt to work on many things at the same time. By allowing ourselves to focus, we reduce or eliminate the cost of context switching. This cost is the invisible enemy of productivity, so the more we can remove it, the more efficient we become. If we have ten projects to deliver, it is proven that if we concentrate on one project at a time, not only will we deliver the first one faster, we will actually deliver all ten before we would have delivered the first one if we worked on all ten at the same time. Ironically, even after running people through an exercise that proves this, they will still insist on having teams or themselves with multiple projects in progress at the same time. This is one we tend to have to continue to come back to in order to help the team refine their priorities until they can routinely focus as much as possible.

Work in Small Batches

By decomposing our work into small pieces, we can better communicate among our team, we can better understand the work that needs to be done, and we can better see that we are making progress towards our goals. All of these benefits help to maintain morale as well as productivity. I have seen teams breaking their stories down into tasks during sprint planning, and then estimating some of the tasks at forty or more hours. I would ask them, how is that breaking the work down? When working at the task level we should strive to have tasks that are a day or less. The smaller we can break the work down the easier it is to share the work amongst the team as well as the quicker the team can show that progress is being made.

The Importance of Trust

In order for Agile to work, there needs to be a strong culture of trust throughout. If the leaders do not trust that the team can follow through on the work, it will be impossible for the team to be fully empowered. Likewise, if everyone on the team is worried that the others on the team are not pulling their weight, it will make working collaboratively extremely difficult. As you can see, trust is a fundamental requirement of working on a strong team.

In his book, *The Five Dysfunctions of a Team,* Peter Lencioni lists the five things that prevent a group of people from truly becoming a team. The first and most important of these dysfunctions is the absence of trust. It is the foundation stone that everything else is built upon. As a Scrum Master, it will be your responsibility to help establish this culture of trust within the team and then to maintain it. In order to help establish this culture, we need to be able to recognize the signs of both a trusting atmosphere as well as a distrusting one.

There are multiple signs of a distrusting culture. The most obvious is when the team is constantly being asked for status updates. Think about this as if you are a manager for a moment. You ask your people to complete an initiative. If you trust them, you will feel confident that they will not only get the job done, but it will be done very well. If you do not trust them, you tend to constantly follow up, asking for status updates, requiring to be told how they plan to accomplish the task and second guessing their approach. Which of these cultures would you prefer to be in as the employee? Which as the manager? It is not hard to see, that not only do we prefer to be trusted, we prefer to trust. So, the question is, if this is the case then why do we often find ourselves in situations where trust does not exist? The opposite of a culture of trust is a culture of fear. The manager requires additional proof because they have been given the impression that failure is not an option; when our future and our careers are dependent on the actions of someone else, it becomes much harder to trust them.

Another sign of the amount of trust is how people and leadership respond to failure. In too many instances, failure is met with repercussions. There is an old saying that I have recently been reminded of.

Mistakes are the only thing we can ever truly call our own. Every success and milestone we achieve is with the help of others, mistakes are ours and unique. It is our responsibility to own them and to learn from them.

~ *source unknown*

When we fully embrace mistakes, when failures are seen as opportunities for learning, then mistakes cease to hold influence on us. If we allow the fear of mistakes to hold us back then we can never reach our full potential, because reaching the stars is never done by playing it safe. It is when we attempt to control everything around us, that the idea of a mistake threatens our ability to "control" our surroundings. However, the truth of the matter is, we only *thought* we had control. The control is an illusion, or like they say in the game of *Portal*, "The cake is a lie". When we accept the reality of mistakes and value them, we are much more likely to try new ideas and experiment.

When we fully embrace this culture of experimentation, we can begin to approach our work processes like scientists. Constantly in the search of truth, we repeatedly try experiments, learning from them, updating our perception of reality and repeating. This empirical process is what allows us to find the innovative solutions to solve our problems and increase our ability to deliver.

When we have a culture without trust, people are less likely to have open and honest communications. However, without these conversations, it becomes difficult to identify the root causes of the issues holding our delivery back. Even if we have a good sense of experimentation, we would not be able to identify the right things to focus on when designing the experiments. It is important to note, that trust is not the only thing that can prevent these conversations. If the company culture is too rooted in politics and saying the wrong thing to the wrong person might get you in trouble, you tend not to say much. When we do have trust and we feel safe, we will be transparent and candid allowing the needed conversations to emerge, even if difficult.

Low trust environments encourage people to do only the minimum required to not get in trouble. This is similar to the movie *Office Space*, when the main character has four different managers give him a hard time for not including a cover sheet on his report. When this happens, people disengage and their morale decreases. Our human resources departments work hard to try and get talented and motivated people, and yet a culture like this destroys their motivation and they either continue to produce lackluster work, or they leave to go to another company that will treat them better. Considering how much it cost the company to replace and retrain people, it is easy to see that it is cost effective to retain our talented people and to replace the people that are only doing the minimum. One of the fastest ways to demotivate your high performers is to tolerate your poor performers. When people see that no one is willing to fix or remove the disengaged people, it pulls everyone down. The opposite of this is also true. When people feel trusted and respected, they will go above and beyond, rising to the challenge and fully engaging in their position. They look forward to coming in to work, and often will work extended hours when needed without burning out. This is different than when they are required to work extended hours to hit an unrealistic deadline. Keep in mind, we do not want to encourage too much of this, but allowing people to follow their passions is something to see.

Servant-Leadership

Servant-leadership is the ability to lead through the act of serving others. There are many roles that can benefit from taking the stance of a servant-leader, among them is the Scrum Master. Since the Scrum Master has no authority to enforce anything, we need to build strong relationships with our teams. There is a phenomenon called the Ben Franklin Effect. It explains a way to quickly encourage someone to like you, even if they didn't know or like you before. The way the effect works is that you find a way to ask the person a favor for you. Because most people like to be helpful, they agree. Their brain then tries to reconcile why they agreed to help you and concludes it must be because you are a friend, or at least on friendly terms. Servant-Leadership is similar to this. We increase the chances that people will value what we say, the more we prove that we are willing to do what we can to help them succeed. There is an important aspect to this which cannot be overlooked. The actions that you take to serve the team must be authentic. If the team sees your actions as inauthentic, they will come to think you are attempting to manipulate them. When your actions are authentic, the team will bond with you. The stronger the bond grows the more you can help coach the team to higher levels of Agile maturity.

There are several ways that a Scrum Master shows this servant-leadership. We will talk about removing obstacles in the next section. This is by far not the only example, but it is an important one. The most common is by being good at facilitating meetings. When the team leaves their meetings feeling that they have been productive, they will come to count on your ability to keep them focused. As you get better at this, it is common for other teams or groups to request you to help facilitate meetings for them. Fulfilling these requests will help you to begin to build relationships with others in the company. You never know when you might have to call on one of these relationships to help your team. Another example is helping the team to push themselves a little so that they begin to achieve more than they thought they could. You could also make sure to celebrate any success the team achieves. The better you can get to know the people, the better you can do small things to let them know you care about them and their successes. Little things begin to build, like remembering the names of their spouses and kids as well as remembering their birthday and celebrating it.

Remove Impediments

As the Scrum Master of the team, it is our main goal to strive to help the team reach their full potential. On the journey towards this lofty goal, there can be many things that can get in the way of the team's progress. We have the difficult job of balancing between removing the impediments and helping the team to know how to take care of the impediments themselves. This can be a fine line and as the team's Agile maturity grows the line continually moves. As we discussed earlier the Shu Ha Ri descriptions will come in handy for this conversation.

When the team is in Shu, you should focus on them shifting to the Agile mindset and adopting the values. In order to allow them to concentrate on those actions while also delivering value, you should attempt to remove any impediments that you can for them. The faster and more thoroughly you accomplish this, the easier it will be for you to gain rapport with the team. This speed is greatly increased as you learn the names of the people that can help you and build those relationships as well. This pays dividends later on and gets the team going in the right direction. The concern comes in if we stay in this position for too long. If we do, the team can start to depend on us in certain aspects. We begin to train them to not do for themselves, which is counter to the direction we want them to move towards. You will sometimes hear this described as someone being a "Scrum Mom". This unfortunate term is attempting to convey the impression of the overprotective parent that will not let their child experience life for themselves because they might get hurt. To this end, it is usually better to err on the side of judging them ready for Ha sooner rather than later.

As the team enters into Ha, and especially as they move towards Ri, we need to start stepping back. We coach them to attempt to handle their own impediments, keeping us informed, so that we can easily escalate if needed. This is an important process since as we step back, the team typically fills in, taking on more self-reliance. What we normally see as we begin this process is that the team will slowly develop their skills and less issues will need to be escalated to you to take care of. For Scrum Masters just learning their role, this can be a scary thought as they feel they will no longer be needed. This is a common misconception. No matter how advanced the team gets, they can always benefit from having a Scrum Master to coach them to stay on track and continue to strive for improvements. As the team handles more of their own impediments, it allows you the time to work with the organization around them to help create a better environment to support the team.

No matter where the team is on the Shu Ha Ri spectrum, there will be some impediments that the team cannot resolve themselves and they need some help with. Some of these you will be able to be resolve and should. However, our power is not absolute. When we cannot solve them, we need to escalate the impediments and work with others in order to get them resolved. There are several different methods that can be used for this depending on the type of impediment and the scaling method being used by the organization. We will talk more about scaling methods shortly. One method of escalation is to go directly to managers or executives that would be able to influence or solve the impediment. This method is especially useful if you are working within a small organization that does not need a scaling method.

In addition to knowing who to reach out to for help and how to escalate issues beyond your control, there is one more important skill you will need to have as strong as possible. This skill is your ability to track the impediments that the team has brought to your attention. This includes the ones you have agreed to resolve and the ones the team has agreed to handle themselves. You will need to be able to give the team updates to let them know you still have this under control, otherwise they will begin to track them as well which is redundant effort. The harder the impediment is to remove the more you will need to communicate to the team that you are still working on it. You will also want to make sure that nothing falls through the cracks and gets missed. This tracking can be done with an impediment board that you keep on your desk or by using the same tool the team uses to track their work. Use whichever approach works the best for you.

Some of the biggest impediments have to do with how the team is setup to begin with. These types of issues are outside of the team's direct control. We will talk about a couple of these as they are as hard to solve as they are common. The first of these issues is when teams that are attempting to work in Agile ways are still required to submit waterfall governance documentation. When this happens, the teams will need to spend more time doing documentation that requires up-front planning more than Agile approaches typically do. This is obviously in direct opposition to the Agile value of "Working software over comprehensive documentation[iii]." Depending on the organization this could take a long time to solve, so make sure you keep the team up to date on your progress.

The rest of the issues we will discuss are based on the composition of the team itself. These composition issues are common during the initial stages of an Agile transformation and can make delivery difficult. Agile teams are meant to be cross-functional and should contain all the skills needed to deliver the work from start to finish. However, sometimes teams are designed to have a group of people with the same skillset. This can be for various reasons, normally when management believes that the "team" should be made up of specialist that they do not have enough of to embed in a bunch of other teams so they design a specialist team that can then support the others. One of the main concerns with this approach is that the teams that depend on this one will not be able to predictably know when they will receive the work as this team will have a different set of priorities from the other individual teams. For the specialist team, this makes their mission harder, as well, as they need to continually context switch in order to work on all the different projects. They will also continually need to play catchup to understand the requests as they were not in all of the design meetings and discussions with the teams. When this pattern is deployed, the specialist team tends to become a bottleneck, preventing the steady flow of delivery. Obviously, this is not something the team can control, so you will need to talk to managers and leaders to see if they will reconsider the implementation of this pattern. Similarly, when a team is made up in such a way that they have too many external dependencies, such as a specialist team or vendors or departments. The number of handoffs required slows down the work, as well as, too be predictable on when the team can deliver the finished value to the customer.

    Teams are also sometimes setup with people not fully dedicated to the team. One of the benefits of Agile teams is that the team members themselves do not have to figure out the priority of the work to be done, they just work on the priority as set by the Product Owner. However, when team members are split across multiple teams, they lose this benefit. If they are split between two teams, then they will need to decide which team's work is higher priority than the other. I was once in a standup with a team which was saying that they were blocked on waiting on something from a member that was only partially on the team. His response floored me. It was along the lines of 'I understand, but this project doesn't pay my salary so the other project needs to get completed first.' This of course is multiplied if they are split across more than two teams. Even for the team members that are dedicated, this becomes difficult to plan for delivery when they do not know how much of their team member's time will be able to be put towards their sprint.

    The last issue can happen even if the team is setup to be truly cross-function, if the managers of the team members do not support that cross-functionality. When this happens, team members will not come out of their specialties. We will talk more about this in Chapter Eight.

    For impediments along these lines, you will need to escalate as their Scrum Master because the team cannot address these issues without outside support. This is when the scaling methods that we touched on earlier come into play. There are several approaches that can be used to scale such as Scrum@Scale, Large Scale Scrum (LeSS), Nexus, and Scaled Agile Framework (SAFe) to name just a few. I will only be going into detail on Scrum@Scale, however you can find plenty of resources on the others if you wish.

Scrum@Scale was created by Scrum, Inc. and has been used in several organizations as a light-weight scaling method. To support escalation and alignment, there are two cycles that are implemented. The first cycle runs through the Scrum Masters. After all teams have had their daily standups, the Scrum Masters of the teams will meet in an event called the Scrum of Scrums, this is sometimes shortened to S2. Any impediments that were unable to be addressed at the team level can be brought up here. Depending on the size of the group involved within the cycle, there could be more than one Scrum of Scrum. When this is the case, there will be a Scrum of Scrum of Scrums or S3. In the S3, representatives from some of the S2 will discuss any impediments that could not be addressed at the S2 level. This method of scaling can be as extensive as needed to ensure that no single event has too many people in it so that it can be completed within the same fifteen-minute timebox that a normal standup event takes. Once the number of teams represented is small enough, the representatives for the Scrum Masters will meet with an Executive Action Team (EAT). This group should be comprised of people that have the authority to remove any impediment raised to this level. In this way, critical impediments can be brought to the attention of senior leadership extremely quickly so that they can be removed as fast as possible. One slight modification that happens often is that in the beginning of this scaling, organizations do not yet see the need to have the scaling events happen every day. They will schedule S2 events weekly, and an EAT event might only happen once a month. This will slow down the ability to respond to your team in a timely manner but will work while you continue to work with leaders to help them understand the cost of delay.

The second cycle is very similar but is comprised of the Product Owners. It scales in much the same way with events called the Meta-Scrum (MS), Meta-Scrum of Scrums (MS2), etc. This series of events will proceed until the Product Owner representatives meet with the Executive Meta-Scrum (EMS). This group should consist of everyone that is authorized to make priority decisions across the organization. With this structure in place, the organization can pivot and adjust very quickly to match the needs of the enterprise. Again, if the meetings are held less frequently, then it slows done the ability to adjust. One common pattern that I have seen with initial implementation of this method is to combine the Scrum of Scrums and Meta-Scrum meetings. There are many reasons that this might be attractive to the organization from a cost saving perspective. The most common is the ease of scheduling when many of the same people would be in both. They are however, separate meetings for a reason. Again, this might be one you have to let go for a while as you coach leadership on the increased benefits of the original design. When this approach is implemented correctly, it will allow organizations of any size to remain in lock-step with itself. This, as you can imagine, is a huge competitive advantage.

Map traditional roles to the Scrum roles

Rear Admiral Grace Hopper said "the most dangerous phrase in the language is: we've always done it this way." The pre-existing role of the Project Manager was originally created so that one person could be ultimately held responsible for the delivery of a solution on a given timeline. This tends to lead to the Project Manager being a task driver, singularly focused on making sure teams execute according to a plan. If the project was late, it is often the Project Manager that is blamed, likewise if it is a success, then they tended to receive the credit regardless of the sacrifices made by the team to achieve it. The common mindset among some Project Managers is that the team is lazy and/or distracted and if not ridden by a strong hand that they will never get the work done on time and that they, as the responsible party, need to be the conscious of the team and keep them focused and working. When the team is on time or ahead, this relationship is normally cordial. However, when the project starts to fall behind, it can become filled with friction. What we have found in the more modern way of working is that people generally want to do good work and try hard to achieve it. When given more freedom to innovate solutions instead of completing tasks, they engage more and become more productive. The team members need to be held accountable to the solution they create and not just a single person.

Before going further, let's stop and discuss the difference between management and leadership. A traditional management approach is to manage or control the people that report to you. You divide up the work and assign it to individual people. You tell the people how to approach and do the work. You also normally keep piling on more work in order to try and control your own workload, until someone eventually breaks under the pressure. Most traditional managers believe that they know how to do the work better that the people doing it and expect to be obeyed without question. To be clear, I am not attempting to say that every manager is this way, but the role was setup this way. There have, especially in recent years, been enlightened managers that have become more leaders than managers as we will describe next.

By contrast, leadership is about empowering the people that report to you. Actually, to be clear, you can be a leader without having people report to you. The expectation is that if you have people reporting to you that you should be a more a leader and less a manager. Leaders know that their people are professionals and treat them as such. They provide direction and allow the individuals the freedom to complete the work. They work on helping their people to develop their skills and refrain from telling their reports what and how to do the work. Leaders also are more in tuned with their reports with a better eye on what is happening in their lives and typically develop stronger relationships with them.

In most traditional organizations people tend to get promoted one step up the ladder past their abilities. They excel at their position for being good at their specialty, so they are promoted to manage others that do that same specialty. The assumption is that if you are good at something, you can help others to become good at it as well. However, just because you are good at something it does not mean that you can mentor others and, it also does not mean that you can manage people, which is itself an entirely different skill set. I remember one time I was working at a retail store and I saw this in action. They had a salesperson that was exceptional, so they promoted her to be a sales manager, and she once again excelled. She was then promoted to store manager and also did a good job. At this point they offered to let her buy the store as a franchise. Even though she excelled at every position up to this point, she had an extremely difficult time running the full store. She got frustrated and started to look for someone to buy the store from her.

With this traditional approach to management, it is no wonder that most teams take their lead from someone in a management position. This person sets the visions as well as assigns tasks, and most of them do not respond well if the team pushes back on the directives. Often, when we are working on transforming a group to an Agile structure and we ask who is the person that understands the customer and has the authority to make decisions about the solution, often the answer is the manager of the people that will be on the team. We tell them that having someone in the Product Owner role that is also the manager can make the team feel disempowered and therefore make the transformation more difficult. Often, this takes a great deal of time and work to change.

In addition to sharing responsibility for the solution with the team, we apply our understanding of limiting your work in progress to reduce the cost of context switching. We see this by the separation of the Project Manager responsibilities between the roles of Product Owner, Scrum Master and the team. This new balance allows for the team to be given a problem to solve and trusts that they will come up with the best possible solution for the customer. It allows the Product Owner to focus on understanding and prioritizing the work for the needs of the customers, and the Scrum Master to monitor and coach on the process to enable the team to improve the way they work.

Some of the most common responsibilities that Project Managers do are:

- Managing the integration with other teams and environment
- Determining the scope of the release
- Setting the timeline for the release
- Handling the financial reporting for the project
- Ensuring the team is delivering a quality solution
- Forming and managing the team that will build the solution
- Handling all communication about the project
- Tracking and mitigating all risks
- Ensuring anything needed for the project is purchased and available

The important thing to note is that whether you are working in traditional waterfall or an Agile way of working, all of this work still needs to be done. One thing that should be clear based on our earlier discussion is that this list is very extensive and requires balancing several different skills simultaneously in order to keep things moving forward. When transitioning to Scrum, we are often asked, who does all this work? The short answer is a lot of different people. The separation of responsibility is to help allow focus and clear delineation of duties. In order to ensure we don't miss anything, let's take them one at a time. You will notice that none of these are placed solely in the hands of a single role. Instead, they are divided up depending upon the scoping of the responsibility.

Managing the integration with other

As we discussed earlier, the Product Owner is responsible for managing dependencies. It then makes sense that they would manage the dependencies for the integration with other teams or departments that might be needed to get a solution rolled out. They will normally need to work with other managers outside of the team to help with setting the correct priority for these shared resources and getting the dependencies aligned.

Determining the scope of the release

This is a good example of splitting a responsibility between multiple roles depending on scope. At the release and initiative level, the Product Owner will determine the scope of the release. In addition, the team will control the scope of the work at the sprint level, controlling how much work they forecast to be done by the end of each sprint.

Setting the timeline for the release

Similar to determining the scope of the work, the Product Owner will set and monitor delivery to the timeline that is needed. The team will determine the timeline for how the work will be done at the sprint level. In addition to this, the Scrum Master assists the team to manage their time, using the processes and working agreements to help them stay focused.

Handling the financial reporting for the project

This is one of the responsibilities I have been asked about the most. The Product Owner handles the financial reporting for the overall initiative. The team is responsible for the estimation of the stories and tasks. This estimation will then be used by the Product Owner to help them determine any changes needed to the financial reporting or timelines.

Ensuring the team is delivering a quality solution

This is the first of these responsibilities that is actually divided up to everyone. The best way to build a quality solution is for quality to be everyone's responsibility. This will include the building of automated tests, defined standards and peer reviews. Part of the empowerment of the team, is for the team to own the quality of the work they deliver.

This shared responsibility also includes allowing the team to have the time to do a quality job and not feel pressured by deadlines to cut corners. By embedding testers within the team, we ensure that the work is tested as soon as possible after the development is completed. This reduces the time and cost of fixing issues. I have often said the true value of embedded quality assurance people in a team is not the testing they do. That is of course important, but the true value is helping to drive that quality mindset throughout the team.

Forming and managing the team that will build the solution

The initial formation of the team is normally done by managers outside of the team. Once the team is established, the team then needs to keep itself accountable for the management on how the team works together. If there is a personality conflict, it will be up to the team to bring up this impediment and see if the makeup of the team can be adjusted to remove the conflict.

Handling all communication about the project

Similar to the quality of the solution, handling communication about the project is everyone's responsibility. There are of course different levels of communication, but it is important for everyone to be as transparent as possible so that we can collaborate as well as we can. Anyone should be able to see the automated reports that whatever tracking tool the team is using. At a previous company that I worked at, they setup a large screen tv at the top of the stairs. This tv continually rotated screens to show the status of every release that was in progress, showing if the releases were on track or behind. We also opened our Sprint Reviews up and invited the whole building at times to stop by and see what was being developed. This type of transparency can only be accomplished when everyone takes responsibility to ensure that the information in the tool is as accurate as possible at all times.

Tracking and mitigating all risks

The tracking and mitigating of risks are also everyone's shared responsibility. The team will need to make sure that everyone is informed of any risks as soon as they are discovered. The Scrum Master and Product Owner will work on mitigation strategies, and the Product Owner will maintain the list of risks so that everyone can see them. Often these risks and/or mitigations will involve coordination with other managers as well. Risks will be discovered during the conversations with the teams. It is important that the Scrum Master is familiar with these risks, as the frequently become impediments that need to be acted on later if the risk manifests.

Ensuring anything needed for the project is purchased and available

The last responsibility that we will talk about is ensuring that anything needed for the solution is purchased. This is typically managed by the Product Owner working in coordination with other managers to ensure the team has what they need for the solution.

This separation and disbursement of responsibilities allows for people to stay focused on the different levels of scope. As you can see, the structure allows for transparency and collaboration to ensure that focus is applied in all the areas. Responsibilities and authority are shared amongst the different roles, and they will sink or swim together.

Grow a Team Culture

Grow a team culture of collaboration and accountability

Once you can establish a good team culture, you will need to maintain and continually strengthen it. In my opinion, this is where a Scrum Master really starts earning their money. No matter how difficult the trip to this point might have been, that was downhill compared to the next leg of the journey. Now we can see the mountain before us. Once the team understands the basics, it becomes our responsibility to bring our hyper-observance to bear and help the team identify where they can make improvements. We are now going to talk about the tools you can use to take the team to this next level.

Al Kraus

Choose your coaching stance

Before I went to my first Coaching Agile Teams class, I thought I fully understood what coaching was. At least coaching in the terms of Agile Coaching. Boy, did I have my eyes opened to how wrong I was. Lyssa Adkins is the author of Coaching Agile Teams and Co-founder of the Agile Coaching Institute (ACI). The Agile Coaching Competency Model created by ACI talks about everything that is needed to be a coach. It includes the strong foundation of lean and Agile principles, the coaching stances we are about to discuss, and then depths of knowledge that different coaches can take. Once taught, the model makes a lot of sense. In my experience, what you will find is that you do not normally stay in any one stance all the time. You will flitter between them as needed with different people and teams. Not only does it take practice to get good at each of these stances, it also takes practice to know which stance to be in at any given time.

Training

Although this sounds self-explanatory, it is worth taking some time to discuss. The skills of being an effective trainer are a discipline onto themselves. One thing that will be required for training is that in order for you to be effective you must know more about the subject than the group you are training. If you find yourself in a situation where you feel training is needed and you do not have more knowledge of the subject, you will be better served to be honest with the team and tell them you will arrange to have someone step in and train them and you. For the most part the training a Scrum Master does is very targeted. Even so, there are some best practices that we will cover.

First, we need to be careful of the presentation we deliver. This is mostly how you approach the training session. Most of the time the training will be on a best practice or process. It is important that we do not give the impression that the team or person is doing something wrong. The training we do is in order to give the team additional information that they might want to use to improve their processes. Like I have said before, we cannot force them to implement this new process or practice. We can explain why the process or practice is recommended and valuable. We also train the team on how to implement it. Ultimately, it will be up to the team if they chose to apply the training for themselves.

Another best practice for our type of training is to train for only seven to at most ten minutes at a time and then have them activate the learning with an activity or exercise. When the training activity takes longer than this, the group starts to lose focus. If you are teaching a full class, there are techniques to change the teaching tools and strategies to allow you to stay within this seven to ten-minute window. By giving the group some kind of activity that they can apply the training that you just put them through, you increase the chances that the training will stick with them.

Mentoring

Mentoring is usually done one on one but can be done in groups as well. Like with Training, you must know more about what you are mentoring on than the person you are mentoring. When you are mentoring, you share your experiences, thoughts, opinions, and ideas with others. This skill attempts to allow the person being mentored to learn from the mentor's experiences. Mentoring can be extremely helpful when trying to get someone up to speed quickly and teaching them the ropes. Even when you are using all of the stances and the person you are working with typically allows you to stay in coaching, you may still need to come back to mentoring if they cannot find their way and need a quick nudge to get going again. It is important to note that the actions that come out of a mentoring session need to be owned and agreed to by the mentee and should not be something you are pushing on them.

I would be amiss if I did not tell you that when done well, mentoring can be an extremely powerful experience. I mentioned earlier that I attended a Coaching Agile Teams training. When I did, I was lucky enough to not only have Lyssa Adkins herself as one of my teachers, but was selected to have a twenty-minute mentoring session with her. Normally speaking, when you are mentoring it is a private conversation in a safe space so that you can have candid conversations. Since it was an example of mentoring, this session was done in front of the entire class of thirty people. All of them sitting on the floor, watching the two of us as we talked. To say that the experience has stuck with me would be an understatement. Shortly after we started talking, I completely forgot about the other people. She asked some extremely powerful questions which helped me understand not only how I felt about the subject but also why I felt that way. She shared her own experiences and then led me to clear actionable steps that I followed up on during the next week. During our conversation, some strong emotions were invoked and there were times I could almost feel tears welling in my eyes; it was that strong of an experience. That has been at least five years ago, and I still remember what she told me, and keep it in my mind on a regular basis.

I hope this illustrates the power that can come from mentoring done extremely well. It is harder to have this level of depth on a regular basis if you are working with the person on a repeating basis. This is mostly because the topics, though important, might not be so near and dear to their hearts to strike this level of emotion. Do not fear though, as you begin to know the person better, you can begin to see what topics they are passionate about and will still have times that you will have the opportunity to be as impactful for them as Lyssa was for me.

Facilitation

We have talked about facilitation already. However, we will be taking a more detailed look into what goes into being in this stance for the team. Similar to how training and mentoring both require you to have context authority in order to be in those stances, both facilitation and coaching require you to have process authority. What this means is that you own the process of the interaction but do not add knowledge directly into the discussion. Professional facilitation requires the facilitator to be neutral and to hold the space and allow the group or person to find their own outcomes. We have often asked a Scrum Master from another team to come in and facilitate release retrospectives for our teams so that we could participate and still have an unbiased facilitator.

Facilitation is about creating an open and safe space to allow the group to find their answers. As I have mentioned, this is done by sharing the rules of the game the group will be playing, asking clarification questions and maintaining the process for them so that they can focus on the topic. It is important that when facilitating, no matter which event you are running, that you keep some of the same skills you use during the retrospective. Keep the conversations focused and help the group drive towards action.

Coaching

Professional coaching is another full skillset by itself. There is also a good deal of people that miss the distinction between coaching and mentoring. Unlike with mentoring, you do not need to have context knowledge. For example, I have never been a recruiter. That means that I would not be able to mentor someone to be a recruiter. I could however, coach someone that is a recruiter and help them discover the answers to their problems. Coaching is definitely a skill that takes a good deal of practice to become proficient at. For me, the hardest part is not slipping back into mentoring. However, I can also attest that the times I have done coaching are much more fulfilling than straight mentoring.

I recommend having a firm grasp on the other stances and the Scrum Master role itself before starting to develop your coaching skills; however, I think it is worth sharing some of the concepts. I will give a high-level overview of a couple of tools here so that you can understand the process. The main tools used for coaching are the arc of the conversation, powerful questions, and active listening.

The arc of the conversation is how you help someone start on their topic, explore the space, and then drive to an action by the end of the time. Here we use powerful questions to help the person see their topic from a different way. This new perspective is what helps them discover a way through their issue. Lastly, active listening. If I am being completely honest, this one is the hardest for me. When I learned this from Lyssa, she referred to this as level two listening which comes from Co-Active Coaching. Level one listening is what we do every day. We listen to others, but at the same time we are thinking about how we will reply, or what we need to pick up on our way home. Level two listening is when you focus on the other person. When they pause, you then take the time to process and respond. This skill of focused listening can be used in many different scenarios. When you first start using this skill you will find yourself repeatedly slipping back into level one listening. It is okay, just refocus yourself on the other person and get back into level two. The more you practice this, they easier it becomes to stay longer in level two listening.

Choosing a Stance

There is an art to being able to choose the correct stance at the right time. It will take time, patience and lots of mistakes until you get good at this critical skill. We will discuss the basics of this decision process, just keep in mind there is a good deal of grey area. As I mentioned, use training in small bursts and only if you feel they can use the process or information in some way very quickly. Scrum Masters will tend to stay most of the time bouncing between the stances of facilitation and mentoring based on the work to be done. Facilitation is the obvious choice whenever you are facilitating a meeting but you can also use it during any discussion with more than two people. Mentoring can be used whenever you are sharing your experiences and opinions. You still want to make sure you are guiding more through questions than directing. You will pull out the coaching stance when the people you are working with have gained experience and should no longer require you to hold their hands. Instead you can use this stance to help them arrive at their own conclusions and directions.

Facilitate the team

When we think of facilitation, we tend to think of facilitating a meeting. However, you can also think of this in a more general sense. The Scrum Master is like a conductor standing in front of the orchestra. It will be your job to help them stay in tune and in time with each other, allowing them to produce beautiful music. When we talk about facilitating the team, this is the mindset we are referring to.

Servant-Leadership

The act of servant-leadership is to lead through empowerment and guidance instead of direct command and control. By building relationships with the team members and helping them to remove their impediments, you will gain influence with them. This influence

> will allow you to guide the team to find their own improvements as well help them adjust the mindset over time.

As we discussed, the Scrum Master coaches the team by being a servant-leader. This comes through in many different ways. One way we have talked about is removing impediments. Impediments by their nature are issues to be resolved. But what if the issue keeps coming back? For example, when the team has an external dependency that causes the work to have to wait while the dependency is resolved. The short-term impediment would be to work with the other team and get the work back as fast as possible. The longer-term solution would be to help the team remove the dependency in some way.

> **Agile Coaching Principle**
> Reduce external dependencies
>
> Anytime the team needs to wait on an external resource, it is not in control of its own delivery. Work on ways to minimize these dependencies and wherever possible eliminate them.

Bruce Tuckman describes four stages of team development. These are Forming, Storming, Norming, and Performing. Teams work through these stages in progression. When first assembled into a team, people tend to be overly polite in order to avoid conflict. This is what is referred to as Forming. After a while, they get tired of suppressing issues as they come to terms that the team will be working together for a while. When they do, they enter the Storming stage. This is typically a time of a great deal of conflict and tense conversations. Once the conflicts are resolved, they move into the Norming stage. This is where they come to terms with how they will best work together. With coaching and time, they can move through Norming into Preforming which is where we see the most return on the investment of establishing the team to begin with. This is why we want to keep teams together as long as possible. Remember that teams will progress through these stages at their own pace. Whenever the team is changed, even by just one person, the team will need to go back forming. Depending on the size of the change, they may quickly catch back up, other times it will take time for them to work their way through.

Understanding the stages of team development, we come to another important service we provide for the team is to help resolve conflicts. Don't get me wrong, in order for a team to become high performing, there needs to be conflict. The trick is to keep the conflict constructive and not destructive. Allowing a team to devolve into name calling and shouting will not help them produce more. Often when tensions run high, having someone there to mediate the discussion helps the conversation remain productive. It is of course easier done when you can detect the issue before it boils up though sometimes this is not possible. It is important that we keep people focused on talking about the issue and not about the person. Helping the team talk things out and find working solutions is what will help the team break through the storming stage and find their normal way of working with each other. This minimizes the length of time they need to stay in this stage of team development.

Managing conflict is not the only way to help build the team. Another great way is to help and encourage the team to have fun. This seems odd to some to talk about work being fun, but we know there is a direct correlation between morale and productivity. This means that the more we can help the team have fun at what they are doing, the more engaged they become. This results in increased productivity.

Agile Coaching Principle
Have fun

Work is work only if you do not enjoy what you do. As much as we strive to be more productive, we also want to have fun and enjoy the journey.

Another useful way to help the team is to help them understand the benefits and value of becoming cross-functional. This helps in many ways. First it helps to ensure that the work does not have to stop if one of the team members is overloaded or on vacation. Second, it encourages team ownership of the work. This is important as when people feel ownership of only part of the work, they tend to disengage from anything not related to what they own. When this happens, meetings become less effective. The point scale that the team uses to size also become less stable as each person maintains their own scale for their work. This in turn decreases the team's overall predictability. When the team embraces cross-functionality and shared ownership of the work, they truly begin to become a team and not just a collection of people. We refer to this as team members being 'T' shaped.

> **Agile Coaching Principle**
> T-shaped members
>
> When a team is made of specialists, we refer to them as having 'I' shaped members. The vertical line of the 'I' represents the deep knowledge they have in a subject area. A team of siloed specialist may seem like it would be the most productive, but becomes unpredictable if anyone is out or the work is unevenly distributed across the team. A team that cross-trains its people to be "T" shaped will be better able to compensate for people being out and in the long run will be more predictable and productive. The vertical part of the 'T' still represents the deep knowledge the member has, but they have gained a broader sense of what the others on the team also do. This cross-training is represented by the horizontal part of the 'T'. This helps remove bottlenecks in the work flow allowing for increase productivity as they continue to work together.

This shared ownership also allows the team to hold itself accountable. This accountability is not only to the work but also to the working agreements they have made to each other. With accountability comes pride. As the team reaches this state with will feel prouder of the work they do and the team they are a part of.

> **Agile Coaching Principle**
> **Team ownership and accountability**
>
> The entire team owns the work done by the team, both for achievement and for maintenance of it. Quality is not owned by the person that tests the work, but by everyone on the team. It needs to be included in every step of the solution not just tacked on at the end. The team needs to hold itself accountable. This extends to each individual as well. As long as they rely on someone else to hold them accountable, they cannot be self-reliant. Without self-reliance, they will not be able to reach their full potential.

Another corner stone of team development is communication. Anything we can do to assist the team to communicate better will help them. It is important to understand that most of the communication between people is not the words we say, but the body language we use as we say it. This is why face-to-face communication is the most complete form of communication.

> **Agile Coaching Principle**
> **Face-to-Face whenever possible**
>
> Whenever possible talk in person. It is the best way to make sure your message is delivered as expected. Email, chat, and video conferencing can work if needed, but are no replacement to face-to-face communication. In the ever increasingly distributed world in which we live, it is important to help the team come up with creative ways to use the tools they have to be as close to face-to-face as possible.

One thing to keep in mind. The longer we continue to coach the team, the more improvements they will be able to find. They will find efficiencies and productivity gains that they never even thought was possible. Continue to push them to think differently and ask what it would take for the impossible to be possible. Both you and they will be surprised at what they can achieve.

Once the team starts to find their rhythm they will eventually and repeatedly start to see their meetings becoming routine and inefficient. You will see this happen a good deal and you should take it in stride. Simply remind the team of why we have that event in the first place. You can also use the 'why' if the team wants to try something different with the meetings. As long as the expected outcome of the event will be achieved, let them try and see if it improves the effectiveness of the meeting. If it does not, you can go back to the way it was. Make sure that you give it enough time to see if you gain the improvement, sometime it takes a while to work out the kinks in trying things a different way.

We have talked about many different ways that you can start to build the team's trust in you. The Scrum Master is often trying to build not only the team's trust in them but also in Agile and Scrum. What I sometimes find is that, as Scrum Masters, we sometimes feel that because we are the experts, the team should just listen to us and do as we say. The thought is that if they trust us that they will likely be happy with the results. However, again it is not about us but about them. We have to earn trust; we cannot demand it. This is also true that Agile needs to build its trust as well. We help to establish this trust in Agile by helping the team discover improvements, asking them to question the way things are currently done and helping them to discover alternatives approaches to the way they work. Celebrate the heck out of any successes that new ideas bring to the team, no matter how small. This begins to build that trust for both you and Agile in general.

There is a big difference between directing a team and coaching a team. Many new Scrum Masters assume that it is their job to direct the team, enforcing the practices of Scrum as well as improvement ideas. Doing this tends to make the team feel that you are belittling them. There are several different ways a Scrum Master can give this impression. It is important to try to avoid as many of these as possible. If we do too many, we can easily become dead to the team, once this happens, we can no longer help them.

Al Kraus

"A dead Scrum Master helps no one."

~ *unknown*

The first common pit fall is to see yourself as an evangelist, preaching the virtues of Scrum no matter what. You can see this when people start sentences like "In the Scrum Guide, it says…". We have talked multiple times about the importance of coaching a team for where they are and not where we want them to be. When you catch yourself using phrases like this, it typically means you are attempting to coach past where the team is on their Agile learning journey. It is best to re-assess where they are and go back to this point.

The better approach is to ask questions. Use the questions to get them to rethink why they do what they do and how they do it. You can use questions to guide the team to a conclusion or idea. This approach allows you an easy out in cases where the idea you had is simply not possible right now for valid reasons. The more we learn about Agile, the team, their environment, the more we will find ways that the team might be able to improve. I recommend that you start recording your observations into a coaching plan. Identify areas that you think are potential improvements for the team. Prioritize your list to identify the improvements that you think will make the biggest impact. Add your observations on why you think the first issue is important. Many Scrum Masters will try to conclude what the root cause of the issue is and what are the best ways to fix it. This is fine to do, but you need to keep it to yourself. I know this is difficult especially if you are like me and are a problem solver at heart. If you tell the team what they have to do to fix an issue, it is less likely that they will buy in to the change. The best approach that I have found is to share my observations in the next retrospective. After sharing the observations, I ask the team if they have noticed these same things. If at this time they say no then you are best served to drop it and ask for ideas from the team. If they have not noticed anything, they likely are not yet ready to address that issue. Move it down in your priority list for later. It might be that now that you have brought their attention to it that they will see similar things through the next sprint and be ready then. If they do say that they have seen what you have, instead of sharing your solutions, ask the team what they think they could do to address the issue. They will sometime come up with a better solution that you did. If they are stuck, you can throw out a hint or two towards your solution and see if they find their way to it. Either way, since they came up with the improvement idea, they are much more likely to buy in and implement it without having to be forced to.

Here are a couple of things to look out for to get you started. First is that the team still sees themselves as a group of individuals and not a team. This can prevent them from understanding why we size as a team or cross train in order to be cross-functional. Another common thing to look for is when the team is not using user stories correctly. This can be for a variety of reasons, like stories are more like tasks, stories are too detailed on the implementation, or the story is too big and vague to actually be completed. Last for this list is when the team has too many external dependencies. This can prevent the team for controlling when and how the work gets done and can take the most effort to address.

Communicate our policies

We will be discussing three main policies that every team should have. I also mention a couple of optional ones that will help us better define our working agreements. It is important to stress that the teams own these policies. Everyone on the team should be accountable to abiding by them and ensure the work meets them. Like we have said, Agile is simple – not easy. It is one thing to state what you want in these policies, but you gain no benefit from them if the team does not honor them. It is better to leave items out than to include something the team will not adhered to.

Working Agreements

It is hard enough to hold a team accountable for policies they have bought into; it is almost impossible to hold them accountable when they have not bought into them.

Explicitly agreeing on and documenting these policies helps a Scrum master stay on firmer ground when attempting to hold the team accountable. This reminds me of a scene in an episode of *How I Met Your Mother*. In this episode, Barney wins an argument. He picks up his phone and pretends to have a conversation with a store. He says, "Hello, leg warehouse? Do you have anything for my friend? No, no leg for him to stand on? Ok thanks." This is why documenting these policies is so important. We never want to be without a leg to stand on. You want that safety net that if you bring something up to the team and they balk on it, you can reply, "You said this is important to you as a team." If it is not important to them, then the policy needs to be updated.

Every team should have a set of working agreements. When helping a team come up with their initial set of agreements, I tend to do something a little different. I set up three columns. The first column I title *Team Alliance*. In this column I ask the team to put words that they want to use to describe how they will work together. I normally start them off with something like "Respectful". Then give them a couple of moments to fill in some more. Then I go to the third column and title it, *Outside Perspective*. I tell them that in this column I want the team to put words to describe how they want everyone else in the company to describe this team. For example, I give them "Dependable". After some time, I move to the middle column. This is titled *Working Agreements*. This one typically requires a bit more explanation before we start in. First, I describe that in this column we what to put the practices and policies that we feel will help make the Team Alliance and Outside Perspective happen. I then explain that in order to be effective the team needs to agree and commit to these policies. The way we decide to keep an idea for the working agreements is a double round of Fist of Five voting. For the first round, I ask the team if they would be okay if someone called them out for breaking the policy in question. If the policy cannot be enforced then it is not worth including. The second round asks the team if they would be willing to call a team member out if they break this policy. If the team is not willing to hold itself accountable it sets the Scrum Master up to be the enforcer of the policy which is a difficult position to be in. If both votes pass, I record the policy into the working agreements. To start the team off, I explain a common agreement called five by five meetings. This policy is to help people to be on time for meetings. It states that meetings will start five minutes after the appointed time, and ends five minutes before the scheduled end time. By doing this people have time to get from their previous meeting and time to get to the next. This is extremely helpful when people have back to back meetings. I explain that this policy helps the team to show respect for each other as well as for others that they work with.

Definition of Ready

Another important policy for the team to make sure they are in agreement on is referred to as the Definition of Ready or DofR. This is a statement of what a user story must have in place in order for it to be considered ready to be brought into a sprint. There are some common points included in the DofR. One of the most common criteria included is that the story meets the INVEST criteria.

INVEST

I – **Independent.** This means that there are no known dependencies that prevent this story from being completed.

N – **Negotiable.** Remembering that the story should be a placeholder for a conversation, you do not want the story so detailed that there is no room for the team to negotiate for a better solution to the request.

V – **Valuable.** The story by itself should have value. This means that you should not have to complete several stories before the customer can see any value.

E – **Estimable.** The story should be clear enough so that the team can estimate the amount of effort required to complete the story.

S – **Sized Appropriately.** The story should be sized by the team and be small enough to be completed within one sprint.

T – **Testable.** The story should contain enough information and acceptance criteria to allow for it to be tested so that a quality solution is developed.

Having a strong DofR is only one part. If the team needs to hold themselves and the Product Owner accountable to make sure that no story is accepted into the sprint if these criteria are not met. Especially for new teams or teams with a new Product Owner, this could be difficult to accomplish. The team needs to be disciplined and stay the course. If they do not, they will be plagued by stories that were rushed through, incomplete and vague, making the development of the work much harder and take longer.

Definition of Done

The last team policy we will talk about is the Definition of Done or DofD. Just as it is important to be explicit on what it takes for a story to be ready to be started; it is just as critical to be explicit on what it means when the team says they are done with it. This policy can be used as a checklist to make sure that all work meets the team's quality standard. Some common items that appear on this policy include:

- ➤ Work has been peer reviewed
- ➤ Story has been verified
- ➤ Story has been accepted by the Product Owner

Similar to the DofR, the team must be disciplined at holding to their DofD. We know that any defect in the work is faster and cheaper to fix the earlier it is discovered and addressed. With this in mind the team greatly reduces the cost of maintaining their quality by building in the quality from the start. It also prevents having to interrupt what they are working on in order to come back and fix something. This will also go towards the team's outside perspective that we already talked about. It is hard to gain the reputation of delivering high quality when you have to frequently come back and fix issues in work that they have declared as done.

It is important that if you have multiple teams sharing a backlog that they should have similar, if not the same, Definitions of Ready and Done. This ensures that the quality of the work and the backlog is maintained in good shape no matter which team pulls the story into their sprint. This will help with overall predictability of the release.

Encourage Team Growth

Encourage teams to push themselves towards improvement

We have discussed multiple ways to start bringing a team together. We will now discuss what it takes to coach a good team to be great. We start moving beyond the team to the environment surrounding them. I have spoken many times about the Scrum Master role being misunderstood. One common misunderstanding is that the Scrum Master should only work with the team. It is true that the team is the focus for the Scrum Master, but many of the best ways to support them is to work with people outside the team in order to help provide the correct environment and support that they need to become great. In this chapter, we will talk about some of the common and difficult issues that can get in the team's way.

Al Kraus

Identify challenges of self-organizing teams

As we start to work with groups of people to attempt to pull them together to be a team, there are a couple of common challenges they can face. We need to be on the lookout for these issues as the root causes are not always easily identified. Once you do identify that one of these issues are present, you will need to work with many different people in order to get it resolved.

We talked before about the three types of motivation: Autonomy, Mastery, and Purpose. This sense of purpose is commonly lost when teams are familiar with a more waterfall approach. Teams are handed detailed plans of what needs to be part of the solution. With the details already defined, it is easy to lose the forest for the trees. What I mean is that when all you have are the details, it is easy to lose track of the big picture. This is why we encourage the user story format that we do, including the why as well as the request. This is also why the Product Owner works with the team daily to speak for the customer. We also recommend using personas to truly drive home the customer focus. Be on the lookout for a team that is losing sight of how their work contributes to the greater whole. This can be an easy fix when identified; however, if not addressed it can kill the team's morale and engagement.

A very common issue is when the team does not feel empowered to make decisions or to own the solution. There can be many different root causes of this issue. First, there could have been a culture of fear, one where mistakes were punished. We talked about this earlier, but it is worth mentioning again because this type of culture can kill any attempt to be more Agile. There could also be a lack of trust by managers that the team is capable of doing the work, so they micromanage in an attempt to keep the work proceeding. This could also be a lack of trust from the Product Owner that the team understands the request and insists in being involved in all design discussions. Lastly, even if the culture and the environment is setup correctly to empower the team, and the team is encouraged and supported to be empowered; until the team steps up to own the empowerment, they are not truly empowered. Empowerment is funny this way, it cannot really be given, however it can definitely be taken away by others. No matter the cause, when the team is not empowered it will be hard for them to find their potential. Having to continually wait for approvals on the approach to take, will cause the team to be plagued with delays. Work with whomever you need to in order to fix this as quickly as possible, it will pay dividends over time.

Similar to empowerment, the team will be held back if there is a lack of a shared ownership of the solution. A typical setup in a waterfall environment is that people own pieces of the solution. They tend to guard their knowledge in order to help protect their positions. When people move from an environment like that to an Agile team, it can be difficult to get them to share their knowledge with the team in order to benefit from the team's ability to deliver value. The problem with a situation like this is that work generally does not come in equal amounts to all parts or skillsets of a cross-functional team. This leads to cases of feast or famine; times when each team member is either only lightly occupied or completely overworked. By sharing the work, we can keep everyone on the team working at a steady, sustainable pace without burning anyone out.

I was once working with a team that worked on mechanical and electrical design and assembly. The manager for the team was explaining to a colleague and myself that his people each owned a release without sharing the work or pairing. The result of this was that each person in turn, when their release was due, would have to work seventy to eighty-hour weeks. This would go on for about a month. After which they would get some "down" time and they would only have to work about twenty hours a week for about a month. We asked the manager if he thought everyone might not be happier just working a consistent forty-hour week and not have to do all the overtime? Believe me, we were surprised when he firmly informed us that he, and by extension his team, liked working this way. Needless to say, we were unable to help him at that time. Some people are just not ready for Agile.

We have talked many times about the importance of helping your team feel like a team. This can sometimes be difficult in a work environment. To quote a previous manager of mine, "If it was easy, everyone would do it." No matter how difficult, you need to bring this group together. Help them to see each other as complete people and not just the skills they have. Host team building events to draw them out and share with each other. People tend to go above and beyond to help people that they care for and respect. So, the more we can bring them together on an emotional level, the more likely they will step up to help each other. And when they do, the sky is the limit. I heard someone say something once and I firmly believe in it as well, though I do not know who to credit for it. If I am given a choice between a team of rock star quality people that cannot work together as a team, or a group of average skilled people that want and can work well together; I will take the latter every time. This is because they will outperform the rock stars in the long run. If you ever doubt this, think of the original dream team. When the opened the Olympics to professional players, a basketball team was form from the greatest players in the NBA. They were all outstanding players, but had difficulty coming together as a team.

Describe importance of technical best practices

No matter what type of work is being done by the team, there are always industry best practices that the team should be doing to ensure the quality of the delivered solution, especially as the team attempts to increase the rate of delivery. Many of these processes require the team to slow down for some time in order to speed up in the long run. What we often find though is the decision to put short term gain ahead of the long-term productivity. The thinking is we will have time to address that later. The reality is that when later comes, we will have something else that is higher priority. With this type of rationalization, the team continues to put off best practices and accumulate more and more technical debt.

> ### Technical Debt
>
> Technical debt is the accumulation of poor design or implementations of a solution. This can be caused through lack of knowledge of a better approach, vastly changing requirements that happen too quickly to address with quality, or time pressure to hit a deadline. Technical debt can come from accidental or deliberate decisions.

I was once working on a team that managed a code base that had method names like "DoTheDonut" and "IgorWrangler". Now method names are supposed to be descriptive so that you have an idea of what they do, however as you can see, these names do not tell you anything about what they do. These are just two examples from a code base littered with methods named similarly. In another code base that we worked with there was a method called "Command Central". This method took in two pieces of information. Based on these two little pieces of information, almost all of the code of the entire application was contained in this one method. You generally try to keep your methods short so that it is easier to see all of it on the screen so you can follow the logic easier. This one method was over sixty thousand lines of code. It made the application extremely difficult to work in and extremely fragile. When code is written like this, it slows the team down as they have to constantly go back and relearn sections of the code whenever they need to make a change or risk inadvertently breaking code in an unknown place.

If teams are not given the time to address technical debt, they will eventually be crushed under its weight. One way to visualize technical debt is similar to financial debt. Picture that each time the team is rushed to a release, it is like adding purchases to a high interest credit card. The longer we put off going back to fix that technical debt, the more interest we have to pay. As we continue to add more debt to the account, we have to pay more and more in interest. If we are not careful, we can get to a point where the interest payment alone is more that we can afford to make payments on. When this happens with technical debt, it become harder and harder to get new features out and eventually forward movement is reduced to a slow crawl.

If you are coming from a non-technical background, some of these concepts might not make complete sense right now. It is okay, if you start working with developers, they will begin to make sense. The important part for now is that you are familiar with the terms and that they are extremely helpful for the team. Part of coaching the team is helping them develop these best practices.

The first group of best practices should in some way or another reduce technical debt and therefore keep production speed as quick as possible. Similar to the first Agile tenet, we will start with the practice of finding a way to visualize the technical debt. It is not good enough for the team members to know what needs to be done. It needs to be visualized in some way so that you can have conversations with the Product Owner to get it prioritized. It is important to prioritize addressing technical debt high on the backlog. In his book, *The Phoenix Project*, Gene Kim says "improving daily work is more important than doing daily work." This is an important break from traditional thinking. It is also critical if we are to get to the point that we want to reach for maximum ability to adjust to changing markets.

It is important to note that there are different levels of technical debt that will need to be addressed. There will be types of technical debt that when found, can be addressed quickly, within an hour or two. This type of technical debt should just be fixed when it is found. No one will notice if the current work is delayed an hour, but if the team takes this as a working agreement, it could be a way of addressing a good deal of the technical debt without any obvious delay to the releases. The next level of debt is something that the team can complete within a couple of days. This type should be written up as a User Story and prioritized on the backlog. The team can work with the Product Owner to bring in one or more of these stories each sprint. The largest level of debt will likely need to be thought of at the release level as it will likely affect release timelines in order to address. Hopefully, anything at this level will be able to be broken down to smaller levels and pulled in to be addressed.

I once had a manager that spoke about large code refactors. He said, "whenever you do a refactor you break something else." So, if this is a common occurrence then how can the team take the risk of doing the refactoring needed to reduce the technical debt? The answer is the next best practice of unit testing. Unit testing is a practice that allows for a series of automated test to be run against the code. Not having unit tests in place is in itself a form of technical debt. Without this, the team will need to spend a large amount of time doing manual testing. A group of teams I was working with once would average about three weeks of manual testing for each of three rounds of submission to a regulatory certification company for each release. As the teams attempted to get up to four releases a year, it became obvious that they would be spending as much time regression testing their application as they were building in new functionality. By adding unit tests, you address technical debt in multiple ways. First, it decreases the amount of time needed for manual testing. Second, it provides a safety net for the team to use when they do refactor projects. This is because if the refactoring breaks anything not intended then the developer knows right away and can fix it quickly. This can be combined with other best practices such as an automated build process which we will discuss in more detail shortly. Thinking back on the example I gave about the teams spending half the year doing testing, if they had this level of automated testing in place, the teams would be able to easily produce twice as much work in a year even if they had not addressed any other forms of technical debt.

With the safety net of automated tests in place, it frees the team up to move faster without fear of breaking the code. This allows them to be more innovative, as well as to constantly be doing small code refactors to improve the code. This can also be taken to the next step which is Test Driven Development. This is a practice where the developers write the unit test before they write the code. Although it may seem like this approach would take longer, the increase in testing speed and the flexibility to try different things without fear, actually allows this approach to be faster for developers. When developers operate without a safety net, they tend to be cautious, making sure that the changes they make will not break anything unexpected. When a net of automated tests is in place, developers can take risks and proceed faster, safe in the knowledge that if anything breaks it will be quickly found and dealt with.

When the automated tests are run whenever the code is committed, it increases the likelihood that the team can truly have a potentially shippable solution at the end of every sprint. The build process we developed when I was working as a developer would run all tests and let us know within minutes if anything failed. It would post in the team's chat room if we committed code that broke anything. It would also continue to notify the channel every ten minutes until we fixed the build process. This type of automated build process can be expanded to become what is referred to as a CI/CD system. This stands for Continuous Integration & Continuous Delivery system. With a fully built system the team can commit code, run it through automated testing, and send it to production within hours instead of having to wait months or more to roll out to production.

There is one last best practice for developers that we will talk about. Feature Toggling is a practice that removes the need to maintain code in separate branches. Using this method allows for a configuration to determine what version of the code should be used. If the feature is not yet complete, it can still be released with the toggle turned off. This helps with integration as well as the reduction or removal of the need of complicated code merges. I have seen teams lose up to three weeks of development trying to complete a complicated code merge.

Whether your team is writing code or doing anything else, there is a general best practice that I believe any team can benefit from. This is the practice of peer reviews. No matter how much we know about the work we are doing, we are still human. Having a second set of eyes looking over the work can vastly improve the quality of the solution created. I recommend this for all teams I work with.

Al Kraus

Serve the Product Owner

A Product Owner can make or break a team. I have seen bad Product Owners completely break a team's momentum and spirit, and seen good Product Owners help to bring the team together. The Product Owner's main responsibility is to understand the customer's wants and needs. They sometimes, however, need a little help to be able to communicate effectively with the team members. Whether or not you have technical knowledge of the work the team is doing, asking a question at the right time can help with this clarity of communication. Product Owners can also use help with the Agile approaches to road-mapping and forecasting. Build a strong relationship with your Product Owner as fast as possible and do everything you can to maintain it. When the Product Owner and Scrum Master are in sync, the team feels supported and encouraged to take flight. When they are opposed, the team starts to doubt and hold back.

Most people that come to the Product Owner role are very knowledgeable about the product or service that the team will be working on but they do not always have knowledge of how to be in this role and how to take advantage of this new way of working with teams. You will need to work with them on how to learn and adapt to this new role. Helping in this way is a great way to create a strong relationship that will help the entire team.

We have already discussed many ways that a Scrum Master can support the Product Owner. We have talked about how we can help by facilitating a Story Jam in order to quickly break down projects or epics to form initial backlogs. We have also talked about how we can help the full team learn how to decompose stories with vertical slices using SPIDR.

Scrum Masters can also help the Product Owner by helping to prepare for the backlog refinement meeting. By helping them to organize their thoughts, filling out the stories and acceptance criteria as best as possible, it will speed up the conversations when the team gets into the refinement meetings. Work with them to send the stories to the team before the refinement meeting and keep all the conversations on track and focused during the meeting.

A great way to help the Product Owner is to help them complete release planning. There are many different ways that we can assist with the process. If it is for a new team without any historic data, we can use a process called Affinity Sizing in order to quickly populate a backlog. This exercise can be done a couple of slightly different ways. This is the way that I typically run it. Like most things, it is easier with some preparation done ahead of time. Create cards with the epics to be included in the release to be planned. Once the team is in the room, I have the Product Owner read each of the epics, giving some high-level overview of what the request is. Once they have been read off. The team can self-organize in order to place the cards into groupings of similarly sized epics. Some facilitators will have the team take turns placing one epic at a time. As each person's turn starts, they could either move an epic that has already been placed or place a new epic. Once the epics have been grouped, we can then ask the team what the relative difference between the groupings are. If unsure, we could use the Fibonacci scale as a reference. Once we have the relative factors, we can ask the team to take an initial attempt to size an epic in the smallest batch. The team should use the same scale that they used for stories. The epic however, will likely have a much larger value than a story brought into a sprint. This SWAG, or scientific wild-ass guess, will be refined as the epic is decomposed into stories that get estimated in later refinement sessions.

Once we have a size on this epic, we can use the relative sizing factors to put SWAGs on the remaining epics. By adding the estimated points on all epics assigned to the release and dividing this total by the average velocity of the team, we can get a rough idea of how many sprints the release might take. If the Product Owner chooses, they could build out a road map of when each epic would be done instead of the release as a single unit. This initial planning can be extremely helpful in allowing the Product Owner to have conversations as needed to ensure that the scope of the release is corrected in order to hit any desired dates. This information may also change the order that the epics are placed on the backlog. This initial relative factor and initial SWAG should be recorded. As the first epic is completed, the Product Owner can use the actual story points for that epic along with the relative factors to have a conversation with the team in order to improve the predictability of the release. It is always better to base the estimation on historical information rather than just a rough guess.

If a team has historical information to begin with, then once we get to the point of having the epics grouped by size, we can compare these to epics the team has previously sized and completed. These size groups rarely only have one epic in them and each completed grouping will have different amounts of points that were needed to complete them. An initial impulse might be to use the average amount of points for the epics in each group. My opinion on this is that if you use the average that means that fifty percent of the time your release plans and road maps will be underestimated. Since so much of this type of planning is being done quickly without all the information, I believe it is better to be pessimistic. Once I know the point range, removing any outliers that are obviously out of range, I take the largest value for the release planning. This increases the chances of the release being delivered on time and even occasionally early.

Earlier we talked about Release Burnups. In order to decrease the noise in the scope line on that report, I have seen teams that will create a placeholder story under each epic with the amount of points identified in the SWAG. As the team decomposes the epic into stories and those stories are sized, we subtract the size from the placeholder. This keeps the scope line steady until the scope actually changes. If we run out of the points on the placeholder, we just put it to zero and keep going. This just means that the epic is taking longer than the initial estimate. New stories added after this will cause the scope line to go up slightly. Once this epic is completed, we will be able to add this information into the historical data so we can get more predictable estimates for our roadmaps in the future. If the work of the epic is completed and the placeholder still has points on it, then we can zero it out and close it. At this point, the scope line for the burnup report will come down, which means we are on track to deliver the release earlier that the initial plan.

It is important that not only do we update the release plans and road maps as each epic is completed but that we also update it at the end of each sprint based on the historic information on the team's performance. As the team's average velocity changes, we get a better idea of when the work for the release is likely to be completed. The hope of course is as the team works together, they can find ways of working more efficiently thus increasing their velocity and their ability to deliver faster.

Every person and company will have a style under stress. This is important to remember. When the team is not directly under release pressure, people tend to have less push back on changing to this new way of working. However, as the release date approaches, people tend to believe that the only way to make it is to revert to more traditional approaches. Often, in situations like this, the Product Owner will try to force the team to pull in more and more work to each sprint in an attempt to catch up to the release plan. It comes from the thinking that the scope and date of the release are fixed and that the team needs to make it happen. This is when you need to keep in mind the iron triangle or iron square whichever you prefer. I tend to go with the square but they both work the same. The triangle has three points of cost, time and scope. The square has the same points and also adds quality. The idea is, using the square, you have time (date), cost (team members), scope (features) and quality; pick three. If an organization pushes date and scope, something else has to give. To have a Product Owner attempt to push a team to commit to more work than they think they can do, only gives an illusion that the work will get done. It is better to encourage the team to take in what they think they can finish and pull in more work if they can get it done. The team should already know the important dates that they are trying to hit. We need to trust the team that they are working as hard as possible to hit the release date. Helping the team to only commit to what they can get done helps in a couple of different ways. First, it shows trust in the team which will help with morale during a stressful time whereas forcing the team to take in too much actually lowers the morale. Second, it guards against the sprint losing importance. If the team is forced to accept in more than they think they can accomplish then when they cannot complete all of it, the importance of the sprint is diminished. The repercussions of this will last much longer than the release itself. This is why it is better to allow the team to only bring in what they are confident of and attempt to complete it. Overcommitting is not going to increase the likelihood of completing the work by the deadline. We should be updating the release plans each sprint so that we can adjust scope in order to hit an important date without having to resort to nights and weekends to make it.

Coach Stakeholders and Leaders

Coach stakeholders and leaders to better support your teams

We know that in order for an Agile culture to really be established, it needs to be modelled and supported at all levels of the company. This includes the senior leadership of the company. The expectations and engagement models have to change if the company wants to get the return on the investment of a large-scale Agile transformation. Just as we need the leaders to model this mindset, we need to ensure that we model it at all times as well. It becomes very difficult to work with others to try to get them to embrace this mindset if we are not modeling it ourselves.

List stakeholder behaviors that support teams

When you first start working with a team, you will find that there are a lot of obstacles and impediments holding them back that are within the team's control to fix. Often what is holding the team back is their belief that they do not have any control. Not everything is within their control, and it is at these times that it is important for the Scrum Master to be able to identify the types of behaviors to encourage in the people interacting with the team to allow the team to succeed.

Experimentation is key to finding valuable improvements to our processes. We talked about this earlier. In order for the team to be comfortable to conduct experiments, leadership needs to accept that sometimes the experiment may be a bit wasteful. As long as we learn from the experiment it was valuable, but it might not always appear that way. When we have tight deadlines, which we almost always do, it can be hard to explain the time investment.

One important aspect of this is to build in slack time into release plans. This extra time can be used in multiple ways. This time can be what is used when experimentation did not produce desired results. It can also be used to add in improvements and automations that the team can do quickly between stories. This time can even be used to provide additional time for training and if no other use is needed, can be used to deliver the solution early if needed. With all those possible uses, the main use for this time is to be able to absorb the time lost from risk mitigation and issues that come up during development. Remember, one of the main things we need to be able to increase is the team's predictability. If we schedule the release without slack time, then if we hit a snag anywhere along the way, the release will be late. Most project management approaches will include some form of buffering to help with this. I propose that they do not add in enough to be able to gain all the advantages listed above. We need to stop assuming that we will be able to get eight hours a day from each person. The only way to get eight hours of work from a person is for them to put in ten to twelve hours a day, and we know that this extra time leads to diminishing returns. It is better to be realistic and only plan for about seventy percent of a person's time towards building a solution.

You are likely asking where I am coming up with this number, so here we go. Ten percent of a person's time is typically taken up by them being a good corporate citizen. Answering emails, walking between meetings, getting coffee, etc. all take up time, though we tend to discount it, but it does add up. Another ten percent is normally taken up by meetings in order to keep the work going. This is if the person is on a Scrum team, if they are working in a more traditional manner it is likely this number will be much higher in order to keep all the statuses up to date. The next ten percent is contested by some, but I stand firm that it is critical. This time should be for each person to continue to improve their professional skills. If we are not constantly trying to get better, our skills dull and we wind up repeating the same approaches over and over instead of finding more efficient ways of working. So, seventy percent should be maximum. There are also other things to consider like, difficult problems that take some time to come up to a solution, as well as, the addition of slack time into the schedule. The good thing about the approach we had for release planning is that if the team creates a habit of incorporating slack time and professional development into each sprint; it will even out in the velocity which will automatically update the release plans.

Another behavior that supports teams is working to improve system throughput. That seems like just common sense, but I must emphasize that this is more important than local efficiencies. An example of local over system efficiencies is when a team focuses on improving the speed of getting code developed as quickly as possible. This is not a bad thing to do, but when you also do not work on automating and streamlining the team's ability to test that code. With this local efficiency, we have more and more code waiting to be tested which typically slows down the overall delivery of value because you increase the time between when a bug was introduced into the solution and when it is discovered. As we talked about earlier this means that it takes longer and cost more to fix. This means that we have to always be thinking of the full system and not just parts of it. A better approach to the above example, would be for the team focus on improving the speed of testing the code first. Once that is in place, then any increases to the development effort will be able to include faster delivery to the customer.

List stakeholder behaviors that do not support teams

There will always be environmental concerns that you will need to be on the lookout for to protect your teams. We have just talked about some of the behaviors that do support the team. It is often even more important to look out behaviors that do not support the teams. This can sometimes lead to having to have some difficult conversations. I once had a manager attend a standup meeting. After the team finished planning their day, she had them go back through the board, task by task. She questioned everything from the time remaining on the task, to who was working on it. It was difficult for me to bite my tongue through all of that. Once the meeting was finally finished, I asked if she had a couple of minutes. I followed her back to the office, shut the door behind me, and took a deep breath. Then started what I knew was going to be a very difficult conversation about the effects of that level of micromanagement. These types of conversations are some of the hardest parts of being a Scrum Master, however they are some of the most important reasons why this role is so critical.

As I mentioned in my story, micromanagement can completely demoralize and kill a team's productivity. We have already talked about how lack of trust can lead to micromanagement. Let's now take a more detailed look on why this can have such a strong negative effect on the team. Most people that are in positions that require problem solving skills do not respond well when told how to do something without room for alteration. The lack of trust comes through loud and clear. Team members start to feel less ownership of the solution and therefore begin to lose their sense of purpose. In one swoop, we send the message that the team is not empowered, that their sense of purpose is reduced, as well as that their autonomy has been taken away. One strong instance of micromanagement, like the one I described in the story, could take months to repair. There are few ways that a manager can damage a team more efficiently than this.

Another behavior that works against the teams is the call to still produce all the documentation and status reporting that was required as part of a more traditional approach. We have talked about release plans and roadmaps. If you are using the right tools to track the work being done, the maintenance of these plans should be able to be generated from the tool. Therefore, removing the need to manually keep track of the team's progress and giving real time access to the current status. If leadership is not content with this level of detail, it will require a good deal of time and energy from the team and especially the Product Owner to create reports and status updates that should not be required. This includes having to have one-off review meetings instead of all the stakeholders coming to the sprint review. This comes from the thinking that it is more important to streamline the time for leadership than for the teams building the solutions. Like I have said often about the Scrum Master role however, it is not about us, but about them. If we want our teams to be as focused as possible, we need to streamline for them and not for leadership.

You have made the observations, and have setup to have one of these difficult conversations. Now what? Well, two of the most powerful tools at your disposal are the use of unintended signals and impact feedback. I originally heard the concept of unintended signals from Daniel Mezick, author and executive coach, during a culture workshop he did for a company I worked for. The idea is you share an observation and then list how that action or words could have been received. The typical reaction is, "I did not mean that." In which you can respond with, I did not say you did, only that it might have come across that way. The way Daniel introduced us to the concept was when he was telling us that being on time is a way of showing respect for others. The president of the company spoke up saying that sometimes it was not possible to be on time, that he frequently had meetings back to back. Daniel, did not reply directly, instead he asked the audience, "When he shows up late to a meeting with you, what thoughts run through your mind?" The response was how we did not matter, the meeting was not important, etc. The president's eye nearly popped out of his head as he replied that he did not mean any of that. Daniel then said, "of course you don't, but the message is still sent anyway." On a side note, this conversation eventually led to a company-wide policy of scheduling meetings twenty-five minutes for the half hour, and fifty minutes for an hour. This allowed everyone time to get to their next meeting on time. This is a powerful technique as you are not telling them they did anything right or wrong, you are just presenting how it might have been interpreted.

I first learned about Impact feedback in my Coaching Agile Teams class. With this technique you specifically mention what effect the word or action had on you. It is important to note, that you can only give impact feedback from your point of view. Unintended signals can be used if you think others were impacted because you are saying that it could have been interpreted that way. Impact feedback is more assertive in that there is no possibility, it did affect you in this way. The format is "when you did or said this, the impact it had on me was…" Impact feedback can be positive and negative. The example I use a lot is that when the people I work with come to me to help them solve their problems, the impact it has on me is that I feel valued and respected.

The benefits to both of these tools are that neither one uses performance feedback. Performance feedback is what we grew up and are used to. It implies that something was done wrong or could have been done better. Most of the time, this approach leads to the person becoming defensive. It also opens the conversation up for debate. This is because you might think I did something wrong, while I disagree and believe I did it right. This quickly becomes a conversation without a winner. However, when we use unintended signals and impact feedback, we can quickly defuse the defensiveness by saying that you are not saying they intended it. It then becomes more of a conversation on what to do, if anything, about the possible misperception. These tools are powerful when helping people to change their mindsets and culture. This is because we often tend to backslide if we are not vigilant. With these tools you can point that out in a constructive and supportive way.

List benefits lost if Scrum is implemented incorrectly

Let me start by asking a question, have you ever been in a position where the business says one thing, but their actions say something completely different? You know that feeling you get when that happened to you? You never know exactly where you stand, you worry about making a mistake. I was once working in a Subway sandwich shop. The owner of the store had been dating the opening manager. I was the store closer, so was the last to leave at night. As such, I was responsible for making sure everything was ready for the morning shift. Everything was fine...until they broke up. Then he would tell me to do things one way, she would tell me another. If I did what he wanted, she blasted me, then I got in trouble for not listening to the manager from the owner. If I did what she wanted, he complained that he was the owner and I should listen to him. It was a no-win situation, at least for me. When we find ourselves in situations like this during an Agile transformation, which happens more than it should, we call it "Agile in Name Only".

You might also hear this referred to as "doing" Agile, not "being" Agile. There is a chasm of difference between the two states of mind of "doing" and "being". More than most recognize.

When we find ourselves in this type of situation, it is important to remember that we need to coach the team for where they are and not where we want them to be. This is a difficult and frustrating place to be for a Scrum Master. That said, we do not want to give up hope. We do need to be able to see the signs and effects of Scrum done incorrectly or incompletely. Teams are required to do the motions of Scrum but without any real sense of empowerment. They are not given the leeway to experiment, so they go through a transformation to a new way of working to replace one ineffective process with another. This is based on the incorrect belief that Scrum will fix all the issues that the organization has. Scrum does not fix problems; it makes the problems visible so that we can fix them. Often this environment is created when top leaders bring in people to do the Agile transformation but the middle managers do not want to actually change. Psychological safety is almost impossible to maintain. Which of course prevents real and difficult conversations from happening. This becomes a self-fulfilling prophecy of going quickly to get nowhere.

The trick when you find yourself in this situation is to be patient. Use your tools and help to slowly change the culture to be more supportive. We have to lead by example, to truly have the Agile mindset we coach people to. Fully embrace the role of servant-leader. This is how a pebble can make ripples that can change the entire pond.

Mentor Others

Improve yourself by helping improve others

Jason Teteak has been training trainers and teachers for over twenty years. He is the author of *Rule the Room* as well as many courses. In his courses, he talks about the five levels of mastery. As trainers we should always strive to have our students to reach at least level four. These levels are:

Level 1: I have no idea what he is doing
Level 2: I see what he is doing
Level 3: I could do that with guidance
Level 4: I could do that without guidance
Level 5: I can teach that to others

It is not my intention to get you from level one to level five through this book. My goal is to get you somewhere between levels three and four. I want you to be able to have confidence in handling the most common aspects of the Scrum Master role. You will still come into situations that you will have to reach out to others for help on ways of dealing with. This could be a coach or another Scrum Master. It is important to make the point that no matter how long you are in this role, you will always occasionally find yourself in a situation where you should bounce ideas off of someone else. This is the nature of the role. However, it also means that as you learn more about the role, there will be other Scrum Masters that come to you for assistance. I am a firm believer that the best way to truly learn something is to teach. So, as you get more into the mentor role, you will find that you are learning as much as you are helping others to learn. As you gain confidence in your ability to own this role, you will find that there are many other people that you will need to help along the way. Let's talk about some of the most common people that you will be mentoring in addition to the team itself.

Mentor Other Scrum Masters

When I was young, I taught myself how to draw. I remember one time when one of my sister's friends saw a drawing I did, she said "I could never draw anything like that." Upon hearing that, I challenged her to a bet. So, in short order we were sitting next to each other with a blank piece of paper in front of each of us. Over the course of the next hour or so, I would draw something on my page like a square or triangle to start. She would draw the same shape on her page. When we were done and she actually looked at what she had done, she had drawn a covered bridge and stone wall with trees on both sides of a river. Without another word she gave me the twenty dollars that we had agreed upon as a bet. I told her, it is not the drawing that is important, it is about learning how to see that is critical.

Similar to drawing, Scrum Masters can be limited based on their ability to see. Whenever I have someone shadow me as a Scrum Master, the phrase I use over and over again is "What did you see?" As an example, upon observing their first standup, when I ask them, they normally give a response along the lines of what the meeting is. I then would ask them if they saw some of the more subtle things about the meeting, like did you notice that when Tim gave his report, he turned his back on Harris? It often surprises them how much detail they've missed this first time. If we do not train ourselves to notice the little things that most people do not see, we will not be able to respond efficiently to issues even before others are aware of the problem. Even if we do not know how to address the situation, if we observe it, we can take the warning signs to someone else for advice and they might be able to help us interpret it. The flip side of this is that if we do not see these things then we have no chance to head the issue off. Hyper-observance, which I introduced in Chapter Three, is a key skill in the Scrum Master toolbox. One of the best things you can do for your fellow Scrum Masters is to help them to gain this skill as well.

Another great thing you can do to mentor other Scrum Masters is to continue to encourage them to learn. I firmly believe that even if I was able to learn for eight hours a day, forty hours a week that I would retire before I learned everything that could make me a better Scrum Master. This is because we pull from so many different fields, each of which is a career path of their own. With so much to learn, to allow ourselves to fall into the trap of thinking we "know" the role and to stop learning is just doing ourselves and our teams a disservice. Helping others to see the benefit of taking the time to continue to learn is a gift they should always appreciate.

I have been working in the Agile space for a long time. As a Scrum Master, I have worked with many teams. I have learned a great deal from these teams and am grateful for the lessons that they have taught me. That said, I have found that I have no greater joy than to help others fulfill their potential. Often, we find ourselves in situations where just talking to someone helps us to see the way forward. Being that sounding post for someone; sharing my experiences and stories to help grow the next generation of Scrum Masters has gotten me through more dark days of frustration then I can count. Listening to another person's issues, gives you a different view of things than when you are experiencing it directly. Our role, unlike many others, is about community and support. It is difficult to be a change agent, and we need to spend time with other change agents so that we can keep our bearings. We sometimes need help in seeing the affect we are having on others. It is too easy to get lost and feel we are adrift and of no value. Sometimes all we get are flickers, candles dancing in the wind to let us know that we are valuable. Sometimes it becomes a spotlight, but often it is just a candle. In times like these we need to be the mirrors to help them turn that candle into a lantern so that they can find their way through. We should always strive to be a lighthouse to help others through their fog, so that when we find ourselves in that same fog, we know where to look for the light from others.

Mentor Non-Agilist

Agile transformation is a cultural shift, not a process or structural one. The process and structure changes are easier to see, but for them to be effective, the culture and mindsets need to shift as well. Every time you have a conversation with someone, share your stories, or support them by answering questions, you help change the culture of those around you. The more seeds of change we can plant, the more chance that they will take root. Imagine an old-fashioned sprinkler system. You know the ones that spray water in one direction then ratchet back to the beginning and start again? I envision this happening whenever I have a conversation with someone. As I talk, they start to align with the Agile mindset. Once they walk away, they ratchet back to their old way of thinking. I see my job as to continue to have these conversations until I can wear out the spring and they stay with the Agile mindset. This is when the curse of knowledge works to our benefit. If we can get them to that ah-ha moment, then they will have difficulty remembering what it was like to think any other way.

Most people that are not currently engaged in Agile ways of working will have little to no idea of what Agile is. I do not know how many times when someone asks me what I do and I tell them I'm an Agile Coach, that they start talking about fitness and gyms and such. I do truly believe the Agile mindset can benefit every person, team, or organization. However, before they can benefit from it, they need to be able to understand it. Learning how to talk about Agile in everyday terms will be invaluable as you work to change the culture around your teams. Most of the time, when I introduce them to the four tenets, they realize that Agile is not some scary new thing. They typically relax as they realize they already are doing some of the tenets and the rest seem to make sense to them.

We also have to lead by example. One of the rules I learned when I owned my own business was it typically takes ten good reviews to make up for one bad one. For us, if we ever slip and act in a non-Agile way, it takes a lot to make up for. Any mistake we make, will likely be brought up whenever we least want it to. So as much as possible, we need to try to be consistent. The good news is that this becomes easier as time goes by.

Engage in the Community

It is very easy for someone that focuses on continual improvement to get overwhelmed by the amount of road in front of them. You begin to feel that "your" company is not doing things correctly; they just don't get it. I was in a situation like this when I went to my first Scrum Gathering. My boss and I were going together, and the whole way there we complained about our company. We listed all the things we were hoping to learn during the convention to help our teams. Over the course of our four days there, our entire outlook changed. It quickly became apparent to us, that although we had a lot of improvements ahead of us as an organization, we were leaps and bounds ahead of many of the others there. We found more and more people coming to us to ask how we had solved this issue or that one because they were facing the same thing. We helped who we could, even as we got help in many ways ourselves. When we returned to work, we still knew that we had a long way to go and we had a couple of new tools to help us get there. We also had more appreciation for how far we had already come. That interaction with the community helped us to balance ourselves and see more objectively where we were on the Agile learning curve. Once there, you can be more present in the moment and a mountain of stress rolled off your shoulders. As important as it is to engage in the community inside your organization, it is even more important to engage in the Agile community at large. Go to conventions, seek out meet ups and user groups. Most areas have Agile communities that meet at regular intervals. Not only will this help you to better master the role, but it also allows you to build networks and connections to help you further your career.

As we have talked about, it is important for every Scrum Master to be active in their community at work. To support each other and learn from each other. This is even more important when it comes to professional advancement. You will need to work with your manager to create a learning journey and career path for yourself. This should always be an ongoing conversation so don't let it only happen at evaluation time. Also remember that as helpful as your manager is in these conversations, you own your own path and need to drive it forward.

Embrace Continual Learning

Improve your own skills and plan for the future.

We have touched on the importance of continuous learning and the amount of information available. In this chapter we will talk more in detail on the different resources available to start you on your learning path. We will also talk about certifications that are available along your journey. We will end with discussing some of the more common career paths that start with the Scrum Master role. You must remember this is not about a destination, it is about the journey itself. We want to keep a direction in mind, but don't forget to pay attention to where you are. Enjoy every step of the journey. All of it will help you to become better, especially during the more difficult times.

Engage in self-study

For a good part of my life, I recharged my batteries by playing games. Mostly video and role-playing games. It is how I would deal with a stressful day or the pressure from finals. While I was working as a developer the stress got so bad that I would escape into World of Warcraft for days. I would spend a couple of hours a night, and my entire weekend playing. That is when I was not working seventy to eighty hours a week to make an impossible deadline. What I have found is that as I have gotten older, I have come to greatly enjoy the idea of continually learning. This idea of knowing a little something more tomorrow than I did this morning is intoxicating to me. I now use learning to recharge instead of games. Don't get me wrong I still play, but it is not the same. I now find that it takes less time in a course or a book for me to recharge than it did while using games to renew. As we discussed in the previous chapter, I believe this is vital for anyone in this line of work. As important as it is to encourage one another, it is even more important to encourage ourselves. It is my belief that everyone should be spending at least ten percent of their time on professional development. Much more for someone just starting out in a Scrum Master role. There is so much to learn, read, and watch in order to be able to better help your teams and your company.

> **Agile Coaching Principle**
> **Continuous Learning**
>
> If we are not continually learning we are falling behind. The only way to stay sharp and increase innovation and creativity is to continually learn new things.

Throughout the course I have made reference to many books and training videos. In the appendix I will have a complete list of all of them to make them easier to make note of. There are a good deal of online classes and videos available as well. There are platforms like Udemy, Edx, and PluralSight that have a great many courses available. Not all of these are worth the time and/or money to do them, but you can find gold among them if you look. Almost every book or course will also give you leads to other books and courses.

When you are thinking of doing research, do not limit yourself to just looking for Scrum Master. You should look for topics like facilitation, coaching, leadership, team building, DevOps, psychology and sociology just to name a few. A great way to engage in your community is to join a book club. YouTube can also be a great reference for you as well. I recommend any videos from Simon Sinek, Lyssa Adkins, and Mike Cohn as a starting point.

Plan for future Certification

The journey of a Scrum Master is like trying to find the end of a rainbow. We can continually make progress, but we can never reach the goal as it moves as we do. I was at a conference once, where Mike Cohn was the keynote speaker. He asked the audience if we had ever watched a show like American Idol or The Voice and seen a truly horrible audition. We all kinda laughed because of course we had. He followed this up with the thought that runs through everyone's mind when they see that, "How did they ever think they could sing?" He goes on to explain that when we only know a little of something, we assume there is only a little more to know about it. As we learn more, we generally begin to understand just how much more there is to know. Hopefully through this book, you have seen a glimpse of what lies ahead of you, not only the breadth and depth of the field before you, but also the support all around you.

Certifications are the milestones that most people look for to show progress. There are definitely some that are table stakes, but they will only get you so far. The knowledge that you learn along the way should always be the true goal. Some of the most recognized certifications for Scrum Master are issued by Scrum Alliance. They are not the only body that offers certification though. Scrum.org also has certification for both Scrum Master and Product Owners. The Scrum.org certification is call Professional Scrum Master (PSM) and has multiple levels. Between the two, I will spend more time on the certifications from Scrum Alliance. The most common and first that someone will go after is the Certified Scrum Master (CSM). There is a common misunderstanding that by having this certification that you are an experienced Scrum Master. Hopefully you now know how much more there is to learn than just a couple of days of training. It is considered by many to be the baseline requirement for the position for most companies. After you have been a Scrum Master long enough, you can go after the Advanced Certified Scrum Master (A-CSM). Along the way, it is helpful to also pursue the Certified Scrum Product Owner (CSPO) as well as this will enable you to better coach the Product Owner. After that, you can continue on to your Certified Scrum Professional (CSP).

There are also other certifications that I believe are definitely worth pursuing. Especially the ones from the Agile Coaching Institute. These are not just for coaches as many of the skills, tools, and techniques are extremely useful to Scrum Masters. Two in particular that had a transformation effect on me are The Agile Facilitator (ICP-ATF) and the Coaching Agile Teams (ICP-CAT) classes. These classes can also be taken as part of a bootcamp which combines both into one event. These classes have likely had more effect on my approach and toolset than most I have taken. Scrum Inc. also has a certification for one of the ways that Scrum can be scaled. The Scrum@Scale Practitioner is a certification for a simple and effective way of scaling Scrum from multiple teams and to entire organizations.

Research the career journeys through Scrum Master

Gone are the days where you would start in a position and have a single path to success. More and more people advance through lattices than ladders. Sometimes you move up, sometimes down, and still other times to the side. All of this in the hope of achieving the position they want, and then they choose the next one to seek. The Scrum Master role is no different, there are many paths through this position, none of them are wrong. I will talk about three of the most common paths. Find the one that resonates with you and follow it. All the while knowing that if later something else resonates with you, you can change focus and move towards it. Nothing is written in stone. Like so many things, enjoy the journey, it is more important than the destination. Once you learn about the different paths, make sure you work with your manager to create a plan that will enable you to reach your goals.

Path of Technical Excellence

This is the most common path and definitely one of the most valuable. This path is for the Scrum Masters that continually sharpen their skills and stays in the Scrum Master role. These are the experienced Scrum Masters that we need to take on more difficult teams and be able to turn them around and increase their productivity. One of my first mentees got so good, that she kept being assigned to the toughest teams in the company. Eventually she asked why she was getting them. I looked at her and said, because you are good enough to help them. Any Scrum Master can excel with an Agilely mature team, but only an excellent one can turn a non-functioning team around. Unfortunately, there are always more teams that need a good deal of work than teams that just run themselves. This is why this path is vital for any organization that wants to sustain an Agile transformation.

Path of Leadership

Being a Scrum Master can be extremely challenging. Especially when it comes to having to have difficult conversations. Being a change agent can create all kinds of waves in an organization. To this end, it is critical to have people that understand the Scrum Master role to be the manager and leader for them. One of the most crucial aspects of the manager is to provide cover and support for the Scrum Masters that report to them. They need to be able to mentor as well as to encourage the Scrum Masters that report to them. Help them to get the training that is needed to make sure the needs of teams and the skills of Scrum Masters are as matched as possible. Different organizations will have different gearing ratios of managers to Scrum Masters. No matter how many they have, it is important that they are ready for the position.

Path of Coaching

The last path we will talk about is the path of coaching. For me, this was the logical next step in the path that brought me to the Scrum Master role. My drive is to help as many people as I can, but as a Scrum Master, I can only help the couple of teams I am working with. This led me to the Agile Coach role. By coaching Scrum Masters and Product Owner to higher levels of efficiency not only do I help them but I also help all the people on their teams as well. This path like all the others has pros and cons. You have to work vicariously through the few who you coach, instead of working with the teams themselves. Going back to the Broadway analogy I mentioned earlier, if the Scrum Master is the stage manager waiting in the wings, the Agile Coach is the trainer that taught the stage manager how to do the job and likely not even in the building while the team is getting their standing ovation.

About the Author

Al Kraus is an experienced Agile Coach and author of *Agile Explained*. He has been in the Agile space since 2006. His mission is to help others feel as fulfilled at work as he does helping them to get there. His credentials include: Certified ScrumMaster (CSM), Certified Scrum Product Owner (CSPO), and Certified Scrum Professional (CSP) as well as a Certified Team Coach (CTC) from Scrum Alliance. Additionally, he is a certified Scrum@Scale practitioner from Scrum Inc. and holds an ICAgile Certificated Professional—Agile Coaching and ICAgile Agile Team Facilitation designations. He is a strong advocate for continual learning and experimentation. Through his tenure at multiple companies, he continues to push himself and his teams for ongoing growth and improvement. Kraus worked as a software developer for years while transitioning to a Scrum Master role. During this time, he also taught night classes at National College in Harrisonburg, Virginia, which fortified his desire to teach others and see them advance. He has been an Agile coach since 2015 and has coached many Scrum Masters and teams.

Building on his credentials as an engaging instructor and facilitator, Kraus created multiple classes aimed at expanding Agile adoption outside the software development and information-technology departments.

Encouraging creativity and a think-outside-the-box mentality, he developed several Agile Community of Practices, along with innovation and technological showcase events.

Kraus has facilitated multiple Open Space events to improve alignment as well as executive strategic-planning meetings. He lives with his wife, Karen, and their daughter, Julie, in North Kingstown, RI. They share their home with their two cats Tessa and Charlie. In addition to his unquenchable thirst for knowledge, he enjoys movies, digital painting, and developing his own computer games.

LinkedIn. https://www.linkedin.com/in/alfredmkraus

References

Scrum: The Art of Doing Twice the Work in half the Time by Jeff Sutherland

The Culture Game by Daniel Mezick

The Scrum Guide by Ken Schwaber and Jeff Sutherland

Scrum Metrics for Hyperproductive Teams: How They Fly like Fighter Aircraft by Scott Downey and Jeff Sutherland

The Five Dysfunctions of a Team by Peter Lencioni

Coaching Agile Teams by Lyssa Adkins

The Phoenix Project by Gene Kim

Rule the Room by Jason Teteak

Photography Credits

Cover Photo by Ameen Fahmy on Unsplash
Chapter One Photo by You X Ventures on Unsplash
Chapter Two Photo by N. on Unsplash
Chapter Three Photo by Yeshi Kangrang on Unsplash
Chapter Four Photo by JESHOOTS.COM on Unsplash
Chapter Five Photo by Ashkan Forouzani on Unsplash
Chapter Six Photo by Riccardo Annandale on Unsplash
Chapter Seven Photo by Guilherme Stecanella on Unsplash
Chapter Eight Photo by Malcolm Lightbody on Unsplash
Chapter Nine Photo by Brandon Green on Unsplash
Chapter Ten Photo by Nicole Geri on Unsplash
Chapter Eleven Photo by Ben White on Unsplash
Chapter Twelve Photo by Elijah Hail on Unsplash

End Notes

[i] Mind-map definition, "What is Mind Mapping?", https://litemind.com/what-is-mind-mapping/

[ii] Mezick, Daniel, *The Culture Game: Tools for the Agile Manager*, 2012

[iii] AgileManifesto.org, *Agile Manifesto*, https://agilemanifesto.org/

www.ingramcontent.com/pod-product-compliance
Lightning Source LLC
Chambersburg PA
CBHW031627210526
45464CB00004B/1780